Additional Praise for SU

*“*Madeleine's many readers will want a copy of SUNCATCHER and then, having read it, will go back and reread their favorite Madeleine books . . . and see them afresh, with more insight into what lies behind the story. By letting Madeleine's life and faith and writing interweave and illuminate each other, Dr. Carole Chase has caught the 'feel' of Madeleine—not just a careful biography but the living person.”

—*Archbishop David Somerville, Vancouver, Canada*

*“*Reflects a beautiful and authentic vision of the person of Madeleine L'Engle. Dr. Carole Chase's biographical research is thorough and reliable; her interpretations of the works of Madeleine show profound understanding.”

—*Rev. Tommy Tyson, Aqueduct Conference Center, Chapel Hill, North Carolina*

*“*Through her exceptionally appropriate metaphor, SUNCATCHER, as title for her book, Carole F. Chase lucidly reveals the various colors of Madeleine L'Engle's life and writings. As she scrutinizes the fiction, poetry, and prose of her honored Suncatcher, she carefully demonstrates how Madeleine beams her metaphorical light squarely into human hearts and society, frequently in words that are disturbing and uprooting, but always in humility and love. Equally unmistakable is her depiction of her Suncatcher's deep belief in the beauty and truth of Scripture, especially the truth of the Trinity, Creation, the Incarnation, and Love. A singular achievement of Carole F. Chase's study is her ability to show how interconnected Madeleine's life, interests, living, and writings are to other human beings and to a changing social order while still remaining a remarkable woman all of a piece. For a balanced and respectful account of Madeleine L'Engle in and through her writings, Carole F. Chase's SUNCATCHER should receive wide attention.”

—*E. Beatrice Batson, Professor Emerita and former Chair of Department of English, Wheaton College*

Suncatcher

SUNCATCHER
SECOND EDITION

A Study of Madeleine L'Engle
and Her Writing

by Carole F. Chase

Foreword by Madeleine L'Engle

Innisfree
Press, Inc.

*A call to the
deep heart's core*

Innisfree Press, Inc.
136 Roumfort Road
Philadelphia, PA 19119-1632

Cover image by Sara Steele.
    "Lake Visions (No Scope Radio)"
    ©1988 by Sara Steele, All Rights Reserved.
    Collection of Marilyn Leventhal.
Cover design by Hugh Duffy.

LIBRARY OF CONGRESS CATALOGING-IN-PUBLICATION DATA
  Chase, Carole F., date.
      Suncatcher : a study of Madeleine L'Engle and her writing /
  by Carole F. Chase ; foreword by Madeleine L'Engle. — 2nd ed.
      p. cm.
      Rev. ed. of: Madeleine L'Engle, suncatcher. c1995.
      Includes bibliographical references and index.
      ISBN 1-880913-31-1 (pbk.)
                                  11. L'Engle,
Madeleine—Criticism and interpretation. 2. Feminism   and literature—United States—History—20th century. 3. Women   and literature—United States—History—20th century. 4. Christian
  literature, American—History and criticism. 5. Spiritual life in
  literature. I. Chase, Carole F., date. Madeleine L'Engle, suncatcher.
  II. Title.
  PS3523.E55Z6   1998
  813'.54—dc21   98-36232
                                                  CIP

Many publishers have generously given permission to use extended quotations from copyrighted works. Permission acknowledgments and copyright
information are listed on page 202.

For Emily

With thanks to Madeleine
for her books, which have inspired me;
for her friendship, which has enriched me;
for her authorization to begin this writing project;
and for the benediction she has given this book.

Works of art are of an infinite solitude,
and no means of approach is so useless as criticism.
Only love can touch and hold them
and be fair to them.

—*Rainer Maria Rilke,* Letters to a Young Poet

CONTENTS

FOREWORD TO THE SECOND EDITION by Madeleine L'Engle 13

FOREWORD TO THE FIRST EDITION by Luci Shaw 17

PREFACE TO THE SECOND EDITION 21

INTRODUCTION: A Project with a Heart 25

   I.   Madeleine, the Storyteller. 29

  II.   The Master Storybook. 45

 III.   The Creator of Galaxies 57

 IV.   Light-Bearers 71

  V.   The Family Table 87

 VI.   Sacred Community 107

VII.   The Butterfly Effect 121

VIII.   Beyond Gender Myths. 137

 IX.   Madeleine, the Mystic. 151

APPENDIX A: Books by Madeleine L'Engle 163

APPENDIX B: The Structure of the L'Engle Corpus. 166

APPENDIX C: A Chronology of Madeleine L'Engle's Life and Books . . .169

APPENDIX D: Madeleine L'Engle's Newbery Medal Award Speech . . .174

APPENDIX E: Families in Madeleine L'Engle's Fiction 179

APPENDIX F: Characters in Madeleine L'Engle's Fiction 184

APPENDIX G: Madeleine L'Engle on the Web 189

NOTES 191

PERMISSION ACKNOWLEDGMENTS 202

INDEX. 205

Foreword
TO THE SECOND EDITION

by Madeleine L'Engle

Why does it give me a feeling of embarrassment to try to write a Foreword to Carole Chase's beautiful book? I suppose because it's about me, and I am seeing myself in a new way. It's a little like walking down the street and seeing the reflection of someone in a shop window, and wondering, "Who is that?" and then realizing with a shock that it isn't a stranger . . . "It's me."

Carole Chase sees me through my books, and that's probably the truest way to see. We also know each other as friends, having been to many conferences together. We have learned over the years that the same things move our hearts: a line in a poem, the sunset spreading across the horizon, the joy in someone's face. But even when we first met, she already knew and cared about my work. Her understanding of what I was hoping to do in my writing warmed my heart.

Carole understands that the work is all of a piece. She has made charts and categories and lists, which are fascinating and useful, but she understands that the whole work is one work: the novels (I started with novels), the science fiction, the poetry, the plays, the young-adult novels, the more meditative nonfiction books. Taken all together, they form an autobiography.

About twenty years ago a young woman came to New York to talk to me because she was writing her dissertation on my work. She announced, "I've divided your work into your early period, your middle period, and your late period."

I responded, "I'm not into my middle period yet."

This is not a mistake Carole Chase has made. She has not been trapped by chronology, either in life or in my work. As I read *Suncatcher*, I am amazed at her insights. As do most writers, I write more than I know. Much writing is done below and above, as well as at the conscious level, and somehow Carole has been able to glimpse all three levels.

My books teach me. I often don't know what I think until I've written it out, maybe three or four times, digging for the truth below the facts. Carole is a truth-seeker, a truth-seeker with a sense of humor. I am grateful that she has been able to see truth in my work, for it is truth that informs my life.

Now that I'm nearly eighty, I look at the work and still see it as a single opus. I hope that life and all that it has taught me has also informed the work, and that I am a better writer now than I was in my early twenties when my first novel was published. It was *The Small Rain*, not, as many people think, *A Wrinkle in Time*. In *Wrinkle*, I was trying to work out what was happening in my life, in my family's life, in the world around me. I did not know that one was not supposed to have a female protagonist in a science fiction book, so perhaps it was my first unconscious affirmation of feminism.

A lot has happened in the world since I made Meg Murry the protagonist of a science fiction book (one of the reasons *Wrinkle* was so slow to find a publisher), and I have been changed by it, as we all have. I gave birth to my first child not long after the United States dropped two atom bombs. Both World Wars changed us. It is still difficult to understand that human beings capable of making music and love and good beef stew could have been part of concentration camps. So any action of love and laughter and compassion strengthens me and gives me hope.

Carole's book gives me hope. When she first talked to me about writing this book, I was honored and happy. I knew that if anyone could see me—Madeleine—with both love and objectivity, it would be Carole.

Later, I told her she was so generous with me that I didn't really recognize the person she was writing about. My friends who have read the book admire it, and admire Carole's insights. I hope, as I continue to write, that I will fulfill her hopes for me and the work.

Foreword
TO THE FIRST EDITION

by Luci Shaw

In the window of my home office, overlooking the garden, hangs a rounded pendant of crystal—clear, faceted, transparent. Suspended as it is from an invisible nylon thread, it turns gently in any imperceptible air that moves in the room. When the sun strikes it, suddenly the white walls and bookcases are flecked with rainbow bits of color. The crystal not only catches the light but refracts it, and as the air turns, the small ball rotates, the multicolored light shifts and penetrates even the darkest corners.

Carole Chase, in naming this welcome book, has perceptively chosen the title *Suncatcher*. She is not just describing a literary theme; she is honoring an extraordinary woman and her writing, which is the subject of the book. The metaphor is entirely appropriate. Madeleine L'Engle's writing—her fiction, reflective prose, and poetry—does indeed cast multicolored reflections of light into the rooms of our lives, not only illuminating them but filling them with dancing iridescence. This combination of clarity and color, light and joy, characterizes the work of this writer in a dark and angry century in which such light, deriving as it does from the light of God, is doubly valuable and treasured.

Carrying the metaphor even further, it seems to me that Carole Chase's examination of the varied motifs in Madeleine L'Engle's writings is her way of allowing each facet to refract its own unique light and color. In giving us this revealing, carefully researched, and penetrating study of Madeleine's themes, Carole has done us all a service. As one who is thoroughly familiar with Madeleine L'Engle's body of work, Carole herself has faceted the reality of this woman she describes as a "suncatcher."

One of the many facets through which God-light is beamed through Madeleine L'Engle is her friendship, for which she has an astonishing capacity. Though she can command large audiences and though her reputation is international, Madeleine remains wonderfully earthy, connected, lacking in hubris, disdaining the pedestal of celebrity on which her devoted public wishes to install her. She loves people one by one.

And she loves God with passion and discipline. Her pattern of morning and evening prayer and Scripture reading keeps her thoroughly in touch with this primary body of truth about God, and gives her the ability to live generatively, that is, spontaneously generating new ideas, new relationships, new explorations, rather than being content to coast or rest on her laurels. This centrality of biblical story in Madeleine's own storytelling is a significant facet of this suncatcher. She knows the Bible not only in its historical detail but viscerally, like the psalmists who let out all the stops of despair and exuberance in their relationship to God. Madeleine has been known to be mad at God, but she also knows the truth of God's loving forgiveness. This overwhelming love of God is perhaps the facet that brightens her writing most persistently and brilliantly.

One of Madeleine's most dazzling abilities is to penetrate the body of scientific writing about, say, quantum mechanics, and extract the core of meaning, like a sweet fruit from its thick husk, in a shape that is both true to scientific principles and yet capable of being understood by non-scientific readers. That such a process is possible is because Madeleine's nuggets of truth are embodied in story. Madeleine's crystal display takes such varied forms as fantasy, science fiction, reflective prose, and poetry, but in all of them, story is her favored medium. The telling of story (which was also Jesus' way of presenting truth) prevents truth from becoming mere abstraction, which may indeed speak to the intelligence but leaves the soul cold, unconvinced, and uninvolved. Madeleine tells stories that speak to the soul and catch us all in the beam of rainbow light.

In that curious and artificial divide between the secular and spiritual worlds, there has long been a dearth of effective interpreters—communicators who can bridge a gap by planting a foot firmly in both worlds and representing each to each with integrity and enthusiasm.

Madeleine L'Engle, as one such mediatrix, has made an astonishing contribution to contemporary culture. The popularity of her books (almost fifty of which are in print—an extraordinary record) and the breadth of her audience, from the very young to the most seasoned reader, demonstrate the level to which she has understood and captured both hearts and minds. She has in truth been a suncatcher—one through whom God-light beams with power enough to illuminate the shadows that persist in both arenas.

I have often seen this light at work. As an editor and publisher who has become a close friend, for over thirty years I have not only been an observer of Madeleine's singular gift of reflective prose and story, I have also been privileged to participate with her in a fervent effort to communicate ideas and stories to a world that badly needs the truth conveyed through idea and story. I have been present at enough public and private gatherings where Madeleine has displayed her wisdom and charisma to marvel at her universal appeal to young and old alike.

Madeleine's high energy is legendary. Carrying her laptop computer and small printer with her wherever she goes, she can be seen at work on planes, in hotel rooms, on trains and freighters, as well as in her bedroom study overlooking the Hudson River or in her office at the Library of the Cathedral of St. John the Divine. Her imagination is at work even when she is separated from her machines. Driving with her through the Canadian Rockies a few years ago, I would notice how, in the middle of a conversation, she would suddenly fall silent and look abstracted; a plot twist or an image for an ongoing story had arrived! She could hardly wait to get back to her hotel room to get it into the computer. And this was supposed to be vacation! For Madeleine, vacation means freedom to write.

Her adventurous spirit is only temporarily deterred by accidents or illness. Whether on a sailboat in Puget Sound, in a zodiac in the Antarctic, on pilgrimage to Iona, or plumbing the depths of a new book on theoretical physics, Madeleine is an explorer and a boundary-breaker. She has also been called a "universe-disturber," but such a term never implies destruction, or malicious disruption. If she shakes up her readers with radical ideas, it is because she is convinced of their truth and necessity, and that, as one who catches light from God, it is her responsibility to beam it into our imaginations.

The question arises: Can any human being adequately represent the truth and light of God? The fact is that God has chosen us humans, flawed and finite as we are, through whom to channel light. George Herbert, the great seventeenth century metaphysical priest and poet, thought so, and wrote:

> How can man preach thy eternall word?
> 　　He is a brittle crazie glasse:
> Yet in thy temple thou dost him afford
> 　　This glorious and transcendent place,
> 　　To be a window, through thy grace.
>
> Doctrine and life, colours and light, in one
> 　　When they combine and mingle, bring
> A strong regard and awe . . . [1]

This poem comes to life in the writing and living of Madeleine L'Engle, one who catches the sun and transmits it to a shadowed world. What an incredible process. What an extraordinary woman!

Preface
TO THE SECOND EDITION

by Carole F. Chase

Trying to keep up with Madeleine L'Engle is like racing with the wind. As I have reread the earliest books and read the seven new books Madeleine has produced since the first edition of this book was published, I have been struck by the image of a single fabric made up of many patterns and pieces.

I am persuaded that most, if not all, of Madeleine's deeply held beliefs may be found like golden threads woven subtly into the patterns of even her earliest fiction. *A Wrinkle in Time* is the exception. It is a golden *cloth*, in which Madeleine's beliefs about good and evil, human freedom, and God are vividly present.

In preparing for this revision, I made a chart of Madeleine's books in chronological order. The result was most interesting. Until 1971, Madeleine had published thirteen books—no small accomplishment. Eleven of these books were fiction, the twelfth was fantasy (the now-famous *A Wrinkle in Time*), followed by a small book of poetry, *Lines Scribbled on an Envelope.*

From 1972 on, the blossoming—or explosion—began. Between 1972 and the present, Madeleine has produced four autobiographical books (now known as the Crosswicks Journals), two books of poetry, a book about the arts, seven books that I have called her personal commentaries on Scripture, four more fantasies, seven novels, a book about religion and art, two picture books of poems and prayers illustrated by her daughter, a book of Christmas writings with Luci Shaw, and a book on friendship with Luci Shaw.

Suncatcher was never intended to be a biography of Madeleine L'Engle. To the extent, however, that she has revealed herself in her writings, shared her vulnerability and her faith with her readers in both fiction and nonfiction, no book about her writing can be separated from the story of her life. Many readers of the first edition of *Suncatcher* felt I was "too generous" and "gentle." I never intended to provide readers with a dry, intellectual, critical analysis of the writings of Madeleine L'Engle. Someday there will be those who approach Madeleine's work with a critical and purely rational eye. This is the way of scholars. It has been, and is, my hope to present a comprehensive summation of the key elements of Madeleine's beliefs and to do this with the same kind of warmth and humanness that characterizes Madeleine's writing.

I hope *Suncatcher* will be useful as a resource for those who read and collect Madeleine's books, and who want to know more about her. On this occasion of celebrating Madeleine's eightieth year, I wish her many more books and workshops and talks, even though this means that I shall forever be trying to "catch the wind."

Acknowledgments

I am grateful to Lou, who suggested the name *Suncatcher* for this book, read the draft, and offered much-needed criticism, suggestions, and support; and to Emily, who listened with ears and heart to a reading of each chapter and who believed in me.

Pam, Vincent, Duchess, and Cassie, whose daily counsel and companionship during our early morning walks inspired me as I journeyed through this project, have earned their place in these acknowledgments.

For her thoughtful Foreword to the first edition, Luci has my gratitude. For her generous Foreword to this revision of *Suncatcher*, Madeleine has my grateful thanks.

I thank Elon College for the sabbatical I was awarded for the fall of 1993, without which this book could not have been born, and for the financial assistance in the summer of 1997 to continue reading Madeleine's papers at Wheaton College.

The list of people connected with the Archives and Special Collections at Wheaton College's Buswell Library who helped in my research must be increased by one. To the names of Mary Dorsett, Larry Thompson, Thad Voss, and David Malone, Judy Truesdale's must be added. Their hospitality, kindness, and consideration not only facilitated my work with Madeleine's papers but helped me locate and substantiate particular details when necessary.

I owe a debt of gratitude to LuraMedia, the original publisher that was willing to take a risk with a green author with the First Edition of *Suncatcher*. As I reflect on the coming together of this revision to celebrate Madeleine L'Engle's eightieth birthday, I am mindful of the hard work of the staff at Innisfree Press on this Second Edition. To Marcia, who alone knows how much her carefulness and hard work have contributed to the integrity of this book, a special word of thanks. The last word is for Kell, my friend. Thank you for the gift of your encouragement, creativity, and imagination.

Introduction
A PROJECT WITH A HEART

We write, we make music, we draw pictures,
because we are listening for meaning, feeling for healing.
And during the writing of the story, or the painting,
or the composing or singing or playing,
we are returned to that open creativity which was ours
when we were children.[1]

In 1984 I suspected that Madeleine L'Engle was a deeply spiritual person. Today, I am certain this is so.

In January 1984, I took a mini-sabbatical from my college teaching responsibilities for the purpose of reading feminist theology and ethics. One day, with my head full of the rational concepts of Mary Daly, Rosemary Reuther, Anne Wilson Schaef, and Beverly Harrison, I picked up Madeleine L'Engle's book *A Ring of Endless Light*.

I was fascinated by this fictional account of a young woman's first encounters with dolphins and with death. The ideas of feminist theology and ethics embodied within its pages—in story form, in right-brain wrapping—came as refreshment to my parched heart.

As I read *Ring,* I moved out of chronological time into one of those rare cosmic experiences of *kairos,* or sacred time. It seemed that the characteristics and concepts of the scholarly material I had been reading were played out before me in a vehicle that made them accessible to my spirit. I was amazed and delighted. I wanted to know more about the ideas and beliefs of this author. I wanted to find out what else she had written and what had been written about her. I wanted to know her!

Recognizing that I had found a path to follow, a project with a heart, I wrote to Madeleine L'Engle:

> I have become exquisitely aware of the fact that your books are woven out of all the themes, ideas, and dreams that make up the best parts of what is in theological, psychological, and sociological fields (to name only a few) being identified as an emerging feminist reality, awareness, energy! This awareness would probably not have zapped in on me so concretely had I not been reading your books at the same time I was reading about the character of the universally emerging feminist consciousness.
>
> I would very much like to do a study of all of your books with an eye to identifying and systematizing and analyzing these materials from a theological and ethical standpoint in general, and from the feminist perspective in particular.[2]

With my reading of *A Ring of Endless Light* and the beginning of my correspondence with Madeleine, I was launched into the study that has culminated in this book. I have since read all of Madeleine's books, attended L'Engle-led conferences and writers' workshops, and developed and taught a religious studies course at Elon College based on her writings. I have visited Madeleine at Crosswicks, her home in Connecticut, and at the Cathedral of St. John the Divine in New York. I have read her correspondence and papers collected at the Buswell Memorial Library at Wheaton College, Wheaton, Illinois.[3] And Madeleine L'Engle and I have become friends.

Because her beliefs are an integral part of her, Madeleine shares them naturally in her autobiographical works and weaves them comfortably into her fantasies and fiction. Certainly Madeleine is an intellectual, but she writes out of an intuitive well overflowing with creativity, imagination, and the experience of eighty years of life.

My purpose in writing this book has been to gather in a systematic framework the essence of Madeleine's spiritual vision that is woven throughout her fiction, fantasy, poetry, autobiography, and personal commentary on Scripture. While I have made no pretense of being objective or critical, I have sought to present and interpret Madeleine's ideas accurately in a personal, friendly, appreciative, and feminist approach.

In *Suncatcher*, I have brought together Madeleine's theology (her words and beliefs about God), her ethics (her understanding of morality), and her spiritual vision (her concept of wholeness for all humanity). My hope is to offer a perspective on the richness of Madeleine's personal faith and spirituality, which she has shared so vulnerably in her stories for over fifty years. I am convinced that the gift of Madeleine's writing is to catch the Light and make it visible for her readers, pointing them beyond her words, beyond Madeleine L'Engle herself, to the realm of the numinous, to the Creator God she worships and seeks to serve.

CHAPTER I

Madeleine, the Storyteller

*We turn to stories and pictures and music
because they show us who and what and why we are, and
what our relationship is to life and death,
what is essential, and
what, despite the arbitrariness of falling beams, will not burn.*[1]

The first time I saw Madeleine L'Engle she was wearing blue jeans. A blue-checkered flannel shirt covered her shoulder and the sling that held her right arm. The jeans and flannel shirt outfit was about all she could wear under the circumstances. She had broken her shoulder in a fall just a week earlier. That was the first and last time I ever saw her in blue jeans.

It was January 1985, and I had arranged to interview Madeleine at the Aqueduct Conference Center in Chapel Hill, North Carolina. We had been corresponding for a year, but this was the first time we were to meet face-to-face, and I was nervous about interviewing this author whose words and ideas had so intensely fascinated me.

During the interview we were both a bit careful because we did not know each other. I asked my prepared questions, and she answered straightforwardly. At the end of the interview, I gave her a booklet containing some of my poetry, and we parted until I returned on Sunday to attend the conference she was leading. When I saw her, she thanked me for the poems and said, "Had I read your poems before our interview, I would have been less nervous."

During that conference, I had an opportunity to witness first-hand Madeleine's warmth, graciousness, and humor as she read from her books and fielded questions from participants. Her appeal clearly lay in who she was as well as in what she was writing and saying. By the time I left Aqueduct, I was deeply moved by the beauty of her spirit and even more convinced of her deep commitment to a God of light and mystery. I was excited about the idea of pursuing my study of this woman and her written and spoken words. I began even then to prepare for this book, to delve deeper into learning about Madeleine's life and her writings.

Certainly, Madeleine L'Engle came by some of her abilities as a deeply intuitive writer from the gifts of inherited creative intelligence and the opportunities of exposure to the arts that her parents gave her while the family lived in New York City. However, other circumstances of her youth and family life also helped to shape the essence of the woman and her creative imagination.

An only child arriving late in the childbearing years of her parents, Madeleine and Charles Camp, she was born November 29, 1918, and baptized Madeleine L'Engle Camp. As a child, she always knew she was loved, but she was left alone a great deal of the time: Her parents did *not* have a child-centered marriage. Madeleine was often sent to her room to eat her supper alone because her mother waited to eat with her father, whose profession of writing play and concert reviews demanded irregular hours. Unhappy at school, where her abilities were not recognized, Madeleine often found pleasure and escape in the private, inner world she created in her room. She wrote her first story at age five and began to keep a personal journal at age eight. Madeleine's fertile imagination bubbled up wonderful ideas for stories, which she captured in writing even as a young girl.

When her father's frail health (the result of permanent lung damage from World War I mustard gas) and their financial situation forced the Camps to live abroad (where the air was cleaner and the cost of living much lower), Madeleine was placed in an English boarding school in Switzerland. The strict Anglican code of behavior and the loneliness she experienced during these years drove her further into her writing and the private, intuitive world of her imagination. She completed high school at Ashley Hall, a private American school in South Carolina, and went on to Smith College, where she majored in English and graduated with honors. She then moved to New York where she took small parts in plays to support herself and "learn about people," while writing stories.

Several of Madeleine's early short stories were published in magazines. She wrote a one-act play, *18 Washington Square, South*, and in 1945 her first book, *The Small Rain*, was published. The protagonist of this first novel was Katherine Forrester, an aspiring concert pianist.

Although there are similarities between Katherine's life and Madeleine's—Katherine Forrester's mother dies, and Madeleine's father had died shortly before she had entered Smith College —Madeleine does not consider the book autobiographical. However, in the introduction to the 1984 reissued edition, she acknowledges,

> My father had died when I was seventeen, and I worked out some of my grief in the death of Katherine's mother.[2]

There are other autobiographical hints, too. Katherine Forrester attended a boarding school in Switzerland and was a lonely and unhappy teenager, just as Madeleine L'Engle had been.

In 1946, the year her second book, *Ilsa*, was published,

Madeleine married actor Hugh Franklin. Their first child, Josephine, was born in 1947. Two more books were published while the Franklins were still in New York: *And Both Were Young* (1949) and *Camilla Dickinson* (1951).[3]

In the early fifties Hugh left acting, and the Franklins moved to Crosswicks, a two-hundred-year-old Connecticut home they had purchased shortly after they married. Their second child, Bion, was born not long after the move. They decided to purchase and run a failing old country store, which added the role of part-time shopkeeper to Madeleine's other roles of wife, mother, and writer. In 1957, Maria, the orphaned seven-year-old daughter of two of the Franklins' best friends, came to live with them at Crosswicks. These years were difficult and stressful for the family, both financially and emotionally. *A Winter's Love* (1957), set in the French Alps, was the only book Madeleine published during this time. She almost gave up writing; she could not seem to get her books published.

On the day Madeleine decided to stop writing, she covered her typewriter and walked around it, weeping. As she wept, she found herself mentally working on a new story about failure. So she uncovered her typewriter. For this, thousands of readers are most thankful.

Three years later, in 1960, *Meet the Austins*, the first of a three-book series, was published. Autobiographical overtones are recognizable in this story of the fictional Austin family. In the first book of the trilogy, the family is joined by Maggy Hamilton, a recently orphaned child, and the story involves the Austin children's dealing with Maggy's arrival. It is also in this book that Madeleine created the first of the three—and only three—characters in all of her stories based on specific individuals in her life. Rob, the youngest sibling in the Austin family, was based on Madeleine's son, Bion. Some, perhaps all, of the prayers Rob offers at the Austin dinner table were Bion's childhood prayers, which Madeleine had recorded in her journals.

After spending almost ten years at Crosswicks, Madeleine and Hugh decided to return to New York and Hugh's acting career. Just before the move, Madeleine, Hugh, Josephine, Bion, and Maria left Connecticut for a ten-week camping trip across the United States. Madeleine used this experience to gather information about traveling and camping, which she later turned into further adventures for the Austin family.

It was during this camping trip that Madeleine got the idea for the three strange beings—Mrs Who, Mrs Whatsit, and Mrs Which—who were to become the angelic beings in what is perhaps her most famous work: the fantasy *A Wrinkle in Time*.

Madeleine completed *Wrinkle* after the family relocated in New York. It was in the writing of this book that she pounded out her own theology, her core beliefs about God, humanity, and the cosmos that she holds today. She also discovered that, for her, writing was not career, but vocation—a sacred calling.

After being rejected by publishers for two years, *A Wrinkle in Time* was finally published in 1962. In 1963, it won the Newbery Medal, a prestigious award given annually since 1922 to an American writer for excellence in children's literature. After that, Madeleine no longer had to worry about finding a publisher. Children and adults wrote to her about the impact of *Wrinkle* on their lives. Her writing career had taken off. The only drawback of the fame and attention the Newbery Medal brought her was being labeled a "children's" writer. She finds that label, like all labels, stifling still.

Settled at last in New York, Madeleine and Hugh sent their children to St. Hilda's and St. Hugh's, an Anglican school in the city, and became involved with teaching in the school's arts programs. Early in the sixties, Madeleine took on the role of official volunteer librarian in the library of the Cathedral of St. John the Divine, which also gave her a place away from home to write. To this day, she continues to go to the Cathedral when she is in New York. There she writes and talks with visitors. •

An early sixties visit to Portugal to do research for *The Love*

Letters (1966) also gave Madeleine fabric for another book, *The Arm of the Starfish* (1965). In *Starfish*, Madeleine introduced Canon Tallis, who was modeled after Canon Edward West of the Cathedral. Canon Tallis is the second of the three characters in Madeleine's fiction based on actual people in her life. Canon West had become Madeleine's spiritual advisor and friend as she worked through her personal religious beliefs and dealt with some of the cosmic questions life had raised for her.[4] When she later mentioned Canon West in her nonfiction writing, she continued to call him "Canon Tallis" because he was more comfortable with the fictitious name.

Madeleine's other books during the sixties included *The Moon by Night* (1963), the second of the Austin novels, describing the family's ten-week camping trip, and *The Young Unicorns* (1968). There were also two biblically-related publications: *The Journey with Jonah* (1967), written first to be performed by students at St. Hilda's and St. Hugh's School in New York, and *Dance in the Desert* (1969), a fantasy symbolic of the Holy Family's escape from Herod.

Madeleine L'Engle's fiction is derived from her own experiences. Indeed, she has said that all of her characters are drawn from herself at various ages. However, it was not until *A Circle of Quiet* (1972) was published that readers had the opportunity to learn the story of her life from a nonfiction source.

This book describes Madeleine's "Crosswicks years" and her struggle to be wife, mother, writer, and sometimes shopkeeper. *Circle* was the first of what has since become known as the *Crosswicks Journals: A Circle of Quiet, The Summer of the Great-grandmother, The Irrational Season,* and *Two-Part Invention.* These nonfiction books, which draw on journals Madeleine has kept since childhood, are rich accounts of her personal faith and philosophy of life.

When Madeleine entered the nonfiction arena in the seventies, she continued simultaneously to produce fiction and fantasies. *The Other Side of the Sun,* a novel about Southern pride and prejudice, was published in 1971. *A Wind in the Door,* the second fantasy continuing her *Wrinkle in Time* adventures, was published in 1973.

The writing of the *Crosswicks Journals* continued with *The Summer of the Great-grandmother* (1974), which covers the last summer of Madeleine's mother's life, a summer Mrs. Camp spent at Crosswicks. *The Irrational Season* (1977), perhaps the most overtly theological of the *Crosswicks Journals,* contains Madeleine's reflections on the church year in both poetry and prose. This was followed in 1978 by *A Swiftly Tilting Planet,* the third fantasy of the series that came to be known as *The Time Trilogy,* which included *A Wrinkle in Time* and *A Wind in the Door.*

The Weather of the Heart, a small volume of lovely poetry, was also published in 1978. Although not usually thought of as a poet, Madeleine has written poetry all of her life. *The Weather of the Heart* states clearly her spiritual faith and her love for Hugh and her family. For readers not familiar with her poetry, the following poem offers a brief taste:

> If thou couldst empty self of selfishness
> And then with love reach out in wide embrace
> Then might God come this purer self to bless;
> So might thou feel the wisdom of His Grace,
> And see, thereby, the radiance of His face.
>
> But selfishness turns inwards, miry, black,
> Refuses stars, sees only clouded night,
> Too full, too dark, cannot confess a lack,
> Turns from God's face, blest, holy, bright,
> Is blinded by the presence of the Light.[5]

In 1975, Professor Clyde Kilby, then curator of the Marion E. Wade Center at Wheaton College in Wheaton, Illinois, invited Madeleine to deposit her papers in the college's Buswell Memorial Library's Special Collections, in which the works of Malcolm Muggeridge and Frederick Buechner are also housed. The Buswell Library is also renowned for its C. S. Lewis Collection.

By the end of the seventies, nineteen of Madeleine's books had been published, including fiction for adults and juveniles, fantasy, autobiography, and poetry.

The decade of the eighties began with publication of the third Austin book, *A Ring of Endless Light* (1980). While it is difficult to choose only one "favorite" of Madeleine's books, this one certainly tops my list. It was this young adult novel that prompted me to pursue a study of her life and writings. Set at Seven Bay Island where the family goes to spend the summer with Mrs. Austin's father, who is dying of leukemia, it is essentially a story about life and resurrection.

By far my favorite of Madeleine's works of fiction marketed for adults is *A Severed Wasp* (1982). If her religious beliefs and views about God and the Gospel were tacit in her earlier fiction, they are overtly displayed in this novel. Katherine Vigneras, nee Forrester, the young protagonist from Madeleine's first novel, *The Small Rain*, has become a world-renowned pianist and retired to New York. Although only thirty-seven "real" years have passed since readers first met Katherine, closer to fifty "fictional" years have passed, and Katherine is in her seventies. The autobiographical parallels continue: Katherine shares Madeleine's love of Bach and, like Madeleine, plays Bach fugues on the piano to relax and work through her worries. Also like Madeleine, Katherine has strong connections with the Cathedral of St. John the Divine, which is the setting for this novel. Felix Bodeway, a retired bishop who served at the Cathedral, asks her to give a benefit concert to raise money for the Cathedral.

Madeleine added another genre to her repertoire in 1983 with the publication of what some refer to as the first book in a trilogy of personal thoughts on Genesis, *And It Was Good: Reflections on Beginnings*. Her disciplined study of the Bible—from her childhood enjoyment of the "stories" of the adventures of biblical characters, to her adult daily pattern of morning and evening Bible reading—bore fruit in this book. In each book of the *Genesis Trilogy*, Madeleine illustrates what she believes the Genesis story reveals about God and humanity.

And It Was Good deals with the first chapters of Genesis, while the second book, *A Stone for a Pillow* (1986), uses the story of Jacob, among other things, to demonstrate Madeleine's conviction that God chooses ordinary people, sometimes even scoundrels, to accomplish God's purposes. The third book, *Sold into Egypt: Joseph's Journey into Human Being* (1989), based on the last chapters of Genesis, has twelve chapters, each devoted to the story of one of Jacob's twelve sons.

During the six-year span over which the *Genesis Trilogy* was published (1983-1989), Madeleine continued to produce fiction and poetry. In *A House Like a Lotus* (1984) and *Many Waters* (1986), she included several characters from *A Wrinkle in Time*.[6]

It was during this period that I first met Madeleine's charming husband, Hugh Franklin. Recently retired from his role as Dr. Charles Tyler in the television series "All My Children," he had accompanied Madeleine to Aqueduct in January 1985 to help her with things she could not do because of her shoulder injury. Because Hugh had come with her, she changed the format of her presentation to include him. I can still picture them sitting in comfortable armchairs in front of a roaring fire reading aloud dialogues from Madeleine's books. This was their first public reading, and they were wonderful together reading the works that Madeleine had birthed.

Since this was their first performance of this type—they had planned it only shortly before arriving at Aqueduct—at times one of them lost the place in the dialogue. Their exchanges, comments, and laughter as they pointed out each other's lapses made the rich, comfortable love they shared obvious to everyone.

After their maiden performance at Aqueduct, the Franklins were invited to read at many places, some of them overseas. The U.S. Information Agency sent Madeleine to Egypt and Austria as a cultural representative. Hugh accompanied her and they continued to read together. The Franklin Christmas letter for 1985 states, "We did readings in Cairo, Heliopolis, Alexandria, Vienna, Klagenfurt, Salzburg." They also gave readings at the University of Connecticut at Storrs, at Calhoun College and Berkeley Divinity School at Yale University, and at Grace Cathedral in San Francisco.

Early in 1986, Madeleine and Hugh made a trip to China. Shortly after their return, Hugh developed a physical problem that turned out to be cancer, and their lives were changed forever. After surgery and one frustrating setback after another, Hugh died in September 1986. After the loss of her husband of forty years, Madeleine wrote the fourth *Crosswicks Journals* book, *Two-Part Invention: The Story of a Marriage* (1988). In graceful prose, she moves between the early years of her life and marriage, and Hugh's illness and death.

For several years after Hugh's death, one or both of her granddaughters lived with Madeleine in her New York apartment while they attended college. In November 1988, her granddaughter Charlotte Jones planned a "surprise" party to celebrate Madeleine's seventieth birthday. The gala party at the Cathedral of St. John the Divine was attended by hundreds of friends and relatives from across the United States.

In 1989, Madeleine published the fantasy *An Acceptable Time*, in which the third character based on a real person in her life appears. According to Madeleine, the character of Bishop Colubra springs from David Somerville, retired archbishop of Vancouver. While she was preparing *An Acceptable Time* for publication, she was also working on the text for *The Glorious Impossible* (1990) to accompany twenty-four paintings by the fourteenth-century Italian painter Giotto on the life of Christ.

Two years elapsed between *The Glorious Impossible* and *Certain Women* (1992), which is perhaps Madeleine's most ambitious work. *Certain Women* takes place in three time periods: the sixties, the decade in which the story is set; flashbacks into the childhood and young adulthood of Emma Wheaton, the protagonist; and the time of the biblical King David. In this play within a play, Madeleine presents a contemporary story parallel with the story of King David, with its entirely different cast of characters. She draws heavily from Hugh's and her own experiences in the theatre and with theatre people. It seems fair to surmise that her experience of Hugh's illness provided a foundation for her portrait of terminally ill, retired actor David Wheaton, the father of Emma Wheaton.

Next came *The Rock That Is Higher: Story as Truth,* published in 1993. Each chapter of this volume elucidates some aspect of story. The reader learns that the "rock that is higher" is neither story nor the Bible, but rather God. This book was written after Madeleine was seriously injured in an automobile accident on July 28, 1991. As she lay in her San Diego hospital bed with time to reflect on her accident and her life, she experienced in a new way the grace of God through friends, family, and the hospital staff, and concluded that her work was not yet done—a conclusion that has since been confirmed many times over by the books she has continued to write.

During a trip to Antarctica in early 1992, Madeleine, the ever-observant traveler, collected notes and ideas that became two new books: a novel, *Troubling a Star* (1994), and *Penguins and Golden Calves: Icons and Idols* (1996). In 1995, Harper SanFrancisco asked me to edit Madeleine's writings into a book of reflections for the calendar year. This book, *Glimpses of Grace,* was published in 1996.

Madeleine's latest novel, *A Live Coal in the Sea,* is a fictional work that pursues the theme of God's grace and forgiveness. Madeleine calls forth Camilla Dickinson, a protagonist from the earlier book entitled *Camilla Dickinson,* who now appears as a college professor with grandchildren.

With the publication of *Anytime Prayers* in 1994, Madeleine added a new type of book to her repertoire: a book of prayers written for children. This book, dedicated to Madeleine's children and grandchildren, is illustrated by photographs of Madeleine's daughter, Maria Rooney.

A second collaboration with Maria Rooney produced the book *Mothers and Daughters*. This 1997 publication includes Maria's photographs of women and girls, mothers and daughters, and is accompanied by a variety of appropriate writings by Madeleine.

Winter Song, a book of Christmas readings by Madeleine and her long-time friend Luci Shaw, was published in time for Christmas 1996. Madeleine's contributions included her previously unpublished Christmas poems.

Her friendship with Luci Shaw prompted Servant Publications to inquire about the possibility of a book co-authored by Luci and Madeleine about their friendship, and friendship in general. The result of this collaboration, *Friends for the Journey*, was published in 1997. An obvious team effort, this book includes dialogue, poetry, and prose by these two long-time friends as they reflect together on friendship.

Madeleine continues to write on a daily basis. One of her recent books, *Bright Evening Star: Mystery of the Incarnation* (1997), offers a set of poetic meditations on the meaning and mystery of the incarnation of God in Jesus. Another recent project is a short book about Moses entitled *Moses, Prince of Egypt: Storyteller's Edition*. She is currently working on a novel about Meg Murry O'Keefe as an adult woman. Many queries come to Madeleine on the whereabouts of Meg's youngest brother, Charles Wallace. At this point, Madeleine says that she doesn't know what has happened to him, but when she finds out, she will write about it in another book.

In honor of Madeleine, and in celebration of her eightieth birthday, Harold Shaw Press published a *Festschrift* titled *The Swiftly Tilting Worlds of Madeleine L'Engle* (1998). This book of essays edited by Luci Shaw was presented to Madeleine in May, 1998. Contributors to this volume are Madeleine's friends and fellow writers: E. Beatrice Batson, Barbara Braver, Thomas Cahill, Alzina

Stone Dale, Myrna R. Grant, Emilie Griffin, Donald R. Hettinga, Thomas Howard, Calvin Miller, Virginia Sten Owens, Katherine Paterson, Eugene H. Peterson, Robert Siegel, Luci Shaw, Walter Wangerin, Jr., and Walter Wink. Before each unique essay, each author pays tribute to Madeleine for her gifts, her friendship, and her unique ability to express profound things of the heart and spirit in exciting, understandable, and inspiring prose and poetry.

For over fifty years, Madeleine L'Engle has been creating out of her beliefs and her life a variegated body of work. Her writings have been studied in college English classes, and journal articles and masters' theses have been written about the literary aspects of her books. Children everywhere know *A Wrinkle in Time*. The public is just beginning to perceive that Madeleine L'Engle is not only a storyteller par excellence, but a teacher about God, humanity, and the cosmos.

One of the best places to discover clues about Madeleine's unique spiritual quality that has so fascinated her readers, as well as the purest distillation of her views about the creative act in general and her writing in particular, is in *Walking on Water: Reflections on Faith and Art* (1980). Here, Madeleine states clearly her belief that all true art is religious, revealing that which is divine, even if the artist does not claim to be religious:[7]

> To be an artist means to approach the light, and that means to let go our control, to allow our whole selves to be placed with absolute faith in that which is greater than we are.[8]

"To let go our control," or "to brush against the hem of the Lord,"[9] is necessary in order for the artist to be part of the creative process. In her storytelling, Madeleine experiences this abandon as she moves out on the other side of time, and of herself. She describes the process as bringing the same joy she feels in her "greatest moments of prayer."[10] For her, praying and writing are linked:

> To work on a book is . . . very much the same thing as to pray. Both involve discipline.[11]

For Madeleine, both writing and praying involve a deep kind of *listening,* moving beyond chatter to the silent place where God can be heard:[12]

> The largest part of the job of the artist is to listen to the work, and to go where it tells him to go.[13]

Then the inspiration comes—*during* the work, during the writing, not before it. Madeleine "listens" to the work she is writing because she believes that the work knows more than she does. She recognizes that when she is deep into her writing, she has moved into an intuitive place beyond the conscious control of her intellect:[14]

> In prayer, in the creative process, these two parts of ourselves, the mind and the heart, the intellect and the intuition, the conscious and the subconscious mind, stop fighting each other and collaborate.[15]

Madeleine believes that the true artist, one who is willing to surrender self, is given the gift of the work.[16] The work, the writing, needs then to be served humbly, regardless of the size of the artist's talent. She considers this act of serving the work "almost identical with adoring the Master of the Universe."[17]

The work, in turn, serves back. Madeleine acknowledges that she learns from her fiction things she would never have learned if she had not opened herself up to them in story:

> Often the events of my life and the events in whatever book I am writing are so inextricably intertwined that I cannot separate them.[18]

In fact, Madeleine would go so far as to say her beliefs are affected more by her stories than her stories are by her beliefs:

> My stories . . . restore me, shake me by the scruff of the neck, and pull this straying sinner into an awed faith.[19]

Writing out of personal need—as Madeleine believes all writers do—she admits that her stories spring "from the writer's need to understand life and all its vagaries and vicissitudes."[20] Her stories provide a means of seeking out answers to her questions about the meaning of life, about the darkness in the world. This search for meaning, which for her is grounded in Scripture, influences the nature of all her writing.

When Calvin L. Porter, professor of New Testament, presented Madeleine at the Christian Theological Seminary in Indianapolis for the receipt of an honorary degree, he said,

> As a writer she invites the stranger into her life and then serves as a priest for those of us who are less articulate, giving expression in words to the struggles, the tragedies, the joys, and the disappointments which all of us experience. She leads her readers into the holy of holies and names for them their own experiences of Divine Reality.[21]

Indeed, Madeleine L'Engle's writing, whether fiction or non-fiction, reveals a lovely light. As I have reflected on the rich variety of books she has produced over more than five decades, the image of a prism, or suncatcher, comes to mind. A prism is a

> transparent material cut with precise angles and plane faces, useful for analyzing and reflecting light. An ordinary triangular prism can disperse white light into a rainbow of colours, called a spectrum.[22]

Imagine, for a moment, Madeleine's body of work as a prism catching the sunlight that we do not literally "see." Just as a prism makes the invisible visible by refracting light into color so, too, do Madeleine's gifts of intuition, imagination, and intelligence, as shared through her stories, catch the Light beyond and make it visible in a rainbow of words, ideas, and emotions.

CHAPTER II

The Master Storybook

The Bible is not objective.
Its stories are passionate,
searching for truth (rather than fact),
and searching most deeply in story.[1]

A lifetime of reading the Bible has profoundly shaped Made-leine L'Engle's spirituality and her writing. Even in her earliest years, the pages of the Old and New Testaments enriched her soul. Although as a child she did not attend Sunday School, her Anglican parents encouraged her to read the Bible. They did not teach her that the Bible was "holy" or "factual," but rather suggested that she read it as a great storybook full of adventures of imperfect people chosen for special deeds and missions. She learned to enjoy finding myth, symbols, drama, history, hymns, and metaphors in its pages. For this future writer, the "master" storybook was a gold mine.

During her two years in an English boarding school, Madeleine found Anglicanism to be too rigid for her spiritual needs, and she abandoned all religious activities—with the exception of what she called "a limited remaining interest in the world of the Bible."[2] In her latter years of high school at Ashley Hall in South Carolina, the environment was more open to the artistic imagination. She writes,

> I regarded much of the Bible as good literature and some of it as bad history. I probably read more Shakespeare than Scripture. At last I was allowed to rejoice in great art.[3]

For Madeleine, college was a time of blossoming. Her Smith College professor, Mary Ellen Chase, whom Madeleine refers to in *A Circle of Quiet* and *The Irrational Season,* advised English literature majors who were considering writing as a profession to become familiar with the Bible in the King James translation because, as Madeleine has told me, it is "the foundation story of the English language."[4] Although Madeleine had rejected the institutional church, she never stopped reading the Bible. But it was under Chase's tutelage that she turned "to the Bible for purely literary reasons"[5] and discovered that the Bible was more "alive" than the institutional church she knew. In its pages she found "joy and piety and history and humor and storytelling and great characters."[6]

It was during her college years that Madeleine developed a daily practice of morning and evening reading of the Scriptures that continues to this day. Later, when she was working and worshipping at the Cathedral of St. John the Divine and holding serious conversations with Canon West about her religious beliefs, she added morning and evening prayer to her daily readings.

She has made it her practice to read through the Bible from cover to cover, "begats and all," in cyclical fashion, starting over again each time she completes the cycle. Some days she reads only a few verses; others, more. In addition to this regular reading, she reads all one hundred fifty Psalms every month, using a morning and evening pattern from the Episcopal *Book of Common Prayer.* Out of this daily study of the Bible, Madeleine has come to know it viscerally. Her thorough knowledge of Scripture, her high regard for its teachings, and her deep understanding of its great stories are reflected clearly in the fiction she has written since the early sixties. Although the primary purpose of her fiction is to tell stories—not to teach readers about the Bible—the theology, the word *about* God, is implicit in her stories. Madeleine's protagonists share favorite scriptural passages with other characters, and, in the Austin series, Bible passages are even painted on the walls.

In *A Wrinkle in Time,* the three children—Meg, her brother Charles Wallace, and their friend Calvin O'Keefe—meet three angelic beings—Mrs Who, Mrs Whatsit, and Mrs Which. Together they "tesser" (time-travel in the fifth dimension) to the planet Uriel. There Mrs Whatsit transforms herself into a white, winged, unicorn-like creature. Riding on the creature's back, the three children make a tour of Uriel. They encounter a field of beasts like the one Mrs Whatsit has become. When the children hear beautiful music and singing they cannot understand, Mrs Whatsit translates for them what turns out to be verses from Isaiah (42:10-12a):

> "Sing unto the Lord a new song, and his praise from the end of the earth, ye that go down to the sea, and all that is therein; the isles, and the inhabitants thereof. Let the wilderness and the cities thereof lift their voice; let the inhabitants of the rock sing, let them shout from the top of the mountains. Let them give glory unto the Lord!"[7]

This biblical passage expresses Madeleine's view of the human need to sing and shout praises to the Creator.

Scriptural quotations appear again in *Wrinkle,* this time spoken by Aunt Beast, a comforting, eyeless creature who nurses Meg back to health after she almost dies in a "tesseract" leaving the planet of Camazotz. Aunt Beast reminds Meg that things seen are temporal; things not seen are eternal (II Corinthians 4:18). Then, when Meg prepares to return to Camazotz to rescue Charles

Wallace, Mrs Who offers the following words from I Corinthians (1:25-28) as a gift to help save her brother:

> "The foolishness of God is wiser than men; and the weakness of God is stronger than men. For ye see your calling, brethren, how that not many wise men after the flesh, not many mighty, not many noble, are called, but God hath chosen the foolish things of the world to confound the wise; and God hath chosen the weak things of the world to confound the things which are mighty. And base things of the world, and things which are despised, hath God chosen, yea, and things which are not, to bring to nought things that are."[8]

Biblical quotations also appear in *The Moon by Night*, the story of the Austin family's ten-week camping trip. Vicky Austin, the main character, puts herself to sleep at night by thinking about a "poem" painted on the walls the loft at their grandfather's house, where the children sleep when they visit him. The poem is actually Psalm 121, which Madeleine includes in its entirety, thus sharing with her readers the words of the Psalm that she so cherishes herself.

Madeleine also gives her characters the opportunity to read Scripture or preach a sermon. This is demonstrated in *A Severed Wasp* when Felix Bodeway, a retired bishop of the Cathedral of St. John the Divine, delivers a sermon the Sunday following the murder of a parish priest, and again in *Certain Women* when Emma Wheaton visits her grandfather, The Rev. Wesley Bowman, and hears one of his Sunday sermons.

In more indirect fashion, Madeleine incorporates Scripture by framing a story in a biblical theme, such as sacrifice, redemption, or forgiveness. Examples of these themes can be found in *A Wrinkle in Time*, *A Ring of Endless Light*, and *A Severed Wasp*, respectively. Sacrifice is demonstrated in an especially obvious fashion in *Wrinkle* when Meg willingly risks her life to save her brother.

A Ring of Endless Light is about resurrection, even though much of it deals with death. The scene in which Zachary Gray talks about his mother, who has recently died, illustrates Madeleine's belief that death never has the last word. Mrs. Gray's body has been "frozen" by a process called cryonics, and Zachary hopes she will be resuscitated sometime in the future when a cure for what killed her is found. Vicky's grandfather, who is dying of leukemia, responds,

> "I think I prefer another kind of resurrection."[9]

When Zachary wonders if Grandfather is concerned about the monetary cost of cryonics, Grandfather reminds him that,

> "Resurrection has always been costly, though not in terms of money. It took only thirty pieces of silver."[10]

Madeleine's conviction that life does not end with death is reflected in this exchange as well as in the renewal and resurrection theme that characterizes the entire book.

Many of Madeleine's works imaginatively transform biblical books into plays or fantasies. Two examples of this occur in *The Journey with Jonah* and *Dance in the Desert*. *The Journey with Jonah* is actually a creative and extended commentary based on the biblical book of Jonah. It might even be considered a modern form of *midrash*—a thoughtful, imaginative commentary on Scripture—in which Madeleine "reads between the lines" without changing the details of the recorded story. Although originally written for high school students and referred to as "a lighthearted one-act play for children,"[11] this play about God's sparing of the city of Nineveh from destruction is also a redemption story that carries a message about the forgiveness and grace of God.

Madeleine has often said that when an idea may be too "difficult" for adults, she puts it into a book for children. In *The Journey with Jonah,* she presents her readers with a story so simple, humorous, and imaginatively written that the message becomes transparent and available not only to children but also to adults whose perceptions may have become clouded.

In a slightly different vein, but also illustrative of Madeleine's art of taking a biblical theme and revealing it in a new way through story, is the lovely fantasy *Dance in the Desert.*

> Once there was a night in the desert where nobody was afraid and everybody danced.[12]

In this story, which may be unfamiliar to many of Madeleine's readers, a mother, father, and infant son seeking to cross the Egyptian desert finally locate a caravan they can join. When night sets in, everything in the desert seems scary and creepy, and the caravan people sit around a fire in the dark. Eventually, one of the camel drivers begins to play a musical instrument. A lion appears at the brow of a nearby dune, and the child approaches the lion. The camel driver takes out a knife, but the mother stops him. The child is not afraid. He approaches the lion, which moves its tail in rhythm with the piper's music. The lion rises on its hind feet and dances. One by one other animals, including a wounded pelican, ostriches, and dragons, come to the child and bow before him. Even a unicorn kneels before the child and then lays its head in the mother's lap. Finally, this strange mixture of real and mythical beasts gathers in a circle around the camp and dances. While they are dancing, the child slips back onto his mother's lap and goes to sleep. The dance ends.

The symbolism in this story is overtly biblical. The father, mother, and infant son certainly are portrayals of the Holy Family escaping across the desert to protect the infant Jesus from Herod's decree of death for all newborns. The safety of the child in the face of the lion affirms the message that perfect love casts out fear. The unicorns, traditionally known to allow themselves to be touched only by virgins, come to the infant's mother. The female pelican, sometimes considered a symbol for God, has drops of blood on it, suggesting the future crucifixion of the man the child is to become. The lack of hostility among the strange beasts is a reminder that, in the presence of the Christ child, there is harmony, unity, and peace. Of course, readers are free to see the child as just a remarkable little boy, but this metaphor/fantasy/story invites readers into a deeper story within a story.

Madeleine also writes poems born out of biblical incidents or based on biblical characters. My favorite of these is based on the story of the woman with an issue of blood (Mark 5:25-34):

> When I pushed through the crowd,
> jostled, bumped, elbowed by the curious
> who wanted to see what everyone else
> was so excited about,
> all I could think of was my pain
> and that perhaps if I could touch him,
> this man who worked miracles,
> cured diseases,
> even those as foul as mine,
> I might find relief. . . .
>
> I stumbled and fell and someone stepped
> on my hand and I cried out
> and nobody heard. I crawled to my feet
> and pushed on and at last I was close,
> so close I could reach out
> and touch with my fingers
> the hem of his garment.
>
> Have you ever been near
> when lightning struck? I was, once, when I was very small
> and a summer storm came without warning
> and lightning split the tree
> under which I had been playing
> and I was flung right across the courtyard.
> That's how it was.
> Only this time I was not the child
> but the tree
> and the lightning filled me. . . .
>
> "Who touched me?" he asked.

I said, "I did, Lord,"
So that he might have the lightning back
which I had taken from him when I touched
his garment's hem.
He looked at me and I knew then
that only he and I knew about the lightning. . . .

He looked at me
and the lightning returned to him again,
though not from me, and he smiled at me
and I knew that I was healed.
Then the crowd came between us
and he moved on, taking the lightning with him
perhaps to strike again. [13]

One of Madeleine L'Engle's gifts is her ability to retell the biblical stories of the cosmos and human existence in ways that are not only easily understood but can also thrill her readers with their power. She reinterprets complex theological concepts into stories, images, and icons that speak to the soul.

Although this ability is evident in both her fiction and her nonfiction works, it is in nonfiction that she demonstrates most overtly her understanding of Scripture. In the *Genesis Trilogy, The Rock That Is Higher,* and her two most recent personal reflections on faith, *Penguins and Golden Calves* and *Bright Evening Star,* she states her views about symbol, myth, revelation, inspiration, and Scripture. In these books the reader learns that Madeleine does not consider the Bible to be primarily a book of moral teachings, but rather a book offering stories of wounded human beings who, in spite of their imperfections, weaknesses, and immoralities, are worthy protagonists. The essence of the Bible, for her, is that God chose then, and chooses now, ordinary people to join in the work of co-creation. She views the Bible as first and foremost a book of "God-stories" about the interactions of human beings with God, stories that tell us "who we are, and who [God] wants us to be."[14]

Ultimately, Madeleine's lifelong love affair with the Bible is a love affair with stories about human beings who are called into relationship with the Creator. She sees the metaphors, symbols, myths, and parables of the Bible as a means of helping finite human beings perceive or describe the infinite. The biblical metaphors invite comparisons; the symbols point beyond themselves to less tangible realities or concepts; and the myths are not untruths, but rather poetic statements of infinite truths:

> Myth is the closest approximation to truth available to the finite human being. And the truth of myth is not limited by time or place. A myth tells of that which was true, is true, and will be true. If we will allow it, myth will integrate intellect and intuition, night and day; our warring opposites are reconciled, male and female, spirit and flesh, desire and will, pain and joy, life and death.[15]

Madeleine considers the Bible a book of great truths by which she seeks to live, but she interprets truth as neither fact nor part of what she calls "the limited realm of literalism."[16] She believes that stories, both biblical and fictional, can be "true" and express deep universal principles without being factual. She also recognizes that truth is frightening and demanding, and lies in the realm of mystery and intuition.[17]

In *Sold into Egypt*, Madeleine reminds us of the meaning of

> *Homo sapiens*, the creature who knows. We know that we know and consequently we ask unanswerable questions.[18]

We humans, she believes, are question-asking beings who have enough intelligence and perspective to sense the wonder of the infinite and ask questions, but not enough to answer our questions based on reason and intellect. As a result, we need myths, symbols, metaphors, icons, and stories to help us understand our questions and the meaning of our existence.

Through stories, she suggests, we can often hear truths we had not recognized before. As she writes in *Sold into Egypt*,

> Jesus did not tell his parables in order to give us facts and information, but to show us *truth*.[19]

Although Jesus' parables offer straightforward messages and can be interpreted on many levels, Madeleine believes that taking them literally squeezes the life out of them. She sees literalism, along with indifference and perfectionism, as killers of story, rendering creativity and imagination impotent. In *The Rock That Is Higher*, she writes,

> How can we understand in terms of literalism the glory of the Creation of the universe, Jonah in the belly of the large fish, Daniel in the lions' den, or angels coming to unsuspecting, ordinary people and crying out, "Fear not!"[20]

Madeleine considers a literal interpretation of the Bible an attempt to tame the wild and wonderful essence of it. She is convinced, for example, that the Genesis stories were designed not only to tell us how Creation happened, but also to open the door for a discussion of ifs and whys.

To illustrate her belief, that while containing truth the Bible must be interpreted as partly myth and fantasy, she points to the story of Ezekiel. Should we take the story of the wheels turning as a factual account of what Ezekiel saw, she asks? Or can we understand it as a wonderful, true—but not factual—statement about the resurrection of the dead?

> To live with an understanding that myth is a vehicle of truth is a far more difficult way to live than literally.[21]

What she finds in Scripture sometimes shocks Madeleine, but she welcomes the shock because it forces her to move into new places of understanding about God and herself. For Madeleine, that limited literalism which demands that the Bible's poetry and story and drama and parable be taken as factual history is one of Satan's cleverest devices. If we allow ourselves to be limited to the known and the explainable, we have thereby closed ourselves off from God and mystery and revelation.[22]

Madeleine's approach to God through Scripture is with awe, not fear.[23] She sees the Bible as a doorway, a window to God that can stretch our concepts of God, if we read it with an openness to

the deeply mythic quality, expressing the longings and aspirations and searchings of the human race.[24]

At the opening of *The Rock That Is Higher*, she quotes a verse from Psalm 61:2 (Coverdale translation):

"From the ends of the earth I call to you,
I call as my heart grows faint;
O set me upon the rock that is higher than I."

This "rock that is higher than I" she interprets to mean faith:

Beneath the reality of life is the rock of faith. I ask God to set me upon a rock that is higher than I so that I may be able to see more clearly, see the tragedy and the joy and sometimes the dull slogging along of life with an assurance that not only is there rock under my feet, but that God made the rock and you and me, and is concerned with Creation, every galaxy, every atom and sub-atomic particle. Matter *matters*.[25]

Madeleine builds on her view of the Bible as a "window to God" in *Penguins and Golden Calves*, a book about icons and idols. She suggests that, when the Bible is taken literally, it becomes an idol, a thing worshipped in itself. In a chapter entitled "The Bible," Madeleine seeks to free her readers from any misconception regarding her views of Scripture. She reveals herself to be a Bible reader who is serious enough to study it daily. She also affirms that she does not take the Bible literally, lightly, or legalistically but rather as an icon that reveals stories about a God of love, forgiveness, grace, and mystery.

Bright Evening Star pursues this idea of mystery:

> When we try to explain it, we lose it. When we try to explain the stories which have grown up around God's love, we lose the love in the midst of the explanations, because love defies explanation. What matters is not whether Adam and Eve were actual, provable, existing people or whether they had belly buttons, but that God in infinite love peopled this lovely little planet for us to care for and expected that we would love each other, and that we would therefore love the God who made it all.[26]

Madeleine urges us not to make idols of the stories themselves but to seek "truth" rather than "fact." In the mystery of the Incarnation, for example, she proposes that, as with the mystery of God's love, finite answers cannot be found in infinite questions.

Through biblical stories Madeleine L'Engle catches glimpses of God and sees more clearly the whole. These stories help her to understand with her heart, to comprehend by faith, the God who created "universes within universes."[27] In her stories, Madeleine invites readers inside the biblical stories, inside themselves, to recognize "God's signature in all of the wonders of creation."[28]

CHAPTER III

The Creator of Galaxies

Oh, I am in awe of the maker of galaxies and geese,
stars and starfish, mercury and men (male and female).
Sometimes it is rapturous awe;
sometimes it is the numinous dread Jacob felt.
Sometimes it is the humble awe
of knowing that ultimately I belong to God,
to the Maker whose thumb print is on each one of us.
And that is blessing.[1]

As a small child, Madeleine L'Engle was taken to visit her maternal grandmother in northern Florida. One lovely, clear night someone took her outside on the beach to see the stars. She has never forgotten this experience of seeing the luminous night world and has named it as her first awareness of the depth and excitement of the universe. Although much of that experience must have been tacit for Madeleine the child, for Madeleine the adult it has made a vast difference. On that starry night, it is likely that author-to-be Madeleine L'Engle Camp not only fell in love with the stars, but also had her first intuitive sense of the Creator who made those stars and flung them into space.

Madeleine grew up believing in God. However, during her difficult Crosswicks years as an adult, she discovered that the God she had found in most churches—an impassive transcendent being —was a God in whom she could no longer believe. She began to search for a God who made sense in a world of suffering, war, and evil.

After failing to find answers to her questions in the writings of contemporary theologians, Madeleine turned to astrophysicists, scientists, and modern mathematicians. There she found a God she could understand and embrace with her intuition and her heart, a God of "galaxies and geese," the Creator of the cosmos. In *Walking on Water*, she writes,

> It was the scientists, with their questions, their awed rapture at the glory of the created universe, who helped to convert me.[2]

Even though Madeleine does not consider herself a theologian, many of her readers do. Since "theology" means, literally, "a word about God," when people study, think, and write about who God is and what God is like, they are in fact being theological.

To expand her knowledge of the Creator, Madeleine turns not only "beyond" to the stars but also "within" as she delves into her daily disciplined study of the Bible. Though she has never been to seminary or taken a graduate degree in religion, Madeleine is extremely well read in both theology and Scripture.

But for all her reading and theological knowledge, Madeleine believes that there is no way the finite human intellect can grasp or describe the infinite, that the rational mind is simply not an effective instrument for understanding God, because understanding God is an affair of the heart and the intuition. But she does believe that we can *begin* to perceive God through imagination; through myths, images, and icons—and, fortunately, for her readers—especially through story.

In her fiction, Madeleine L'Engle presents a Creator God who is intimately involved in human affairs. In *Meet the Austins* we are introduced to Grandfather Eaton, Vicky Austin's maternal grandfather and a minister.[3] In a dinner scene, Madeleine's view of God briefly flickers into sight as the family members hold hands around the table for grace:

> Grandfather said in a voice loud and glad:
> "Oh come, let us sing unto the Lord,
> Let us make a joyful noise to the rock of our salvation,
> Let us come before His presence with Thanksgiving,
> And make a joyful noise unto Him with psalms."[4]

In another conversation, again at the dinner table, the discussion turns to God and science. When Vicky's brother John states that Albert Einstein did not believe in God, Grandfather excuses himself from the table and returns with a book. He reads Einstein's own words, which declare his profound faith as a scientist in an intelligence that the harmony of the universe reveals. These words, as read by Grandfather, further impart Einstein's conviction that in the presence of this superior intelligence the proper attitude of the scientist is "rapturous amazement."[5]

In this passage Madeleine underlines her appreciation of the awe with which great scientists such as Einstein view the Creation. In the description of Grandfather's bedroom, we get another glimpse into her view of God. Painted on the wall is this inscription:

> "God is over all things, under all things; outside all; within, but not enclosed; without, but not excluded; above, but not raised up; below, but not depressed; wholly above, presiding; wholly without, embracing; wholly within, filling."[6]

Since Madeleine invented the character of Grandfather, it is reasonable to assume that his favorite quotations also have meaning for her. These words of Hildevert of Lavardin, a twelfth-century Catholic mystic, provide additional clues about

Madeleine's concept of a God who is both a part of every person's life and unlimited by time and space.[7]

Grandfather Eaton is a believer after Madeleine's own heart: He is devout yet open-minded, he is also an admirer of Einstein, and his concept of God is not confined to a closed system. While Madeleine claims that if any character in the Austin series is modeled after her, it is Vicky, it is clear that there is also a significant bit of Madeleine in Grandfather.[8]

In the second of the Austin books, *The Moon by Night*, a character named Zachary Gray appears. Zachary is a cynical and apparently atheistic young man. His heart has suffered damage from rheumatic fever, and he has a rather careless and fatalistic attitude about his life. He finds Vicky Austin attractive and pops up at various camp sites as the family travels west on their ten-week camping trip. One night, he takes Vicky to see the play *The Diary of Anne Frank*. After the play, over sodas, they have a serious discussion about God, humanity, and the meaning of life. Vicky/Madeleine tells the story of the play, including the scene in which Mrs. Frank prays for God to prevent the Nazis from discovering the Jewish family's hiding place. But the family is not saved. Vicky and Zachary are grappling with the seeming unfairness of life, as if for the first time.[9]

The next day, Vicky pursues the topic of life's unjustness with her Uncle Douglas. Madeleine uses this conversation to reveal some beliefs of her own. Realizing that Vicky is upset, Uncle Douglas reminds her that her grandfather, while fully aware of the wickedness and apparent injustice in the world, continues to have a calm faith and a firm belief that God is a loving God.[10]

Madeleine puts into Vicky's mouth these words of doubt:

> "If God lets things be unfair, if He lets things like Anne Frank happen, then I don't love Him, I hate Him!"[11]

Perhaps Madeleine is speaking here out of her own disappointment that God does not prevent pain, loss, and rejection in life. Yet, like Grandfather, Madeleine has continually sought after God in the midst of heartache. She relates that some of her most honest conversations with God have taken place during difficult times of her life, walking alone down the dirt lane at Crosswicks.[12]

In response to Vicky's outburst, Uncle Douglas delivers a mini-lecture about human freedom, which he believes causes much of human pain. For God to interfere every time we choose to make a wrong move would violate human freedom, he tells her.[13] He compares searching for answers to the mystery of God to doing a jigsaw puzzle: We can only see a few of the pieces. He tells Vicky that by faith we believe there is a whole puzzle and that it is complete.[14] Vicky listens but is still not persuaded.

Later, at another camp site, Zachary and Vicky wander off. Zachary gets trapped inside a cave formed by a rock slide. It grows dark, and after Vicky has called out for help to no avail, Zachary persuades her to leave him and go for help. But the rock slide has so changed the landscape that Vicky cannot find her way in the dark, and she returns to Zachary's "prison." Sitting outside the cave and warmed by Zachary's jacket, Vicky recites Psalms to comfort herself (just as Madeleine herself does), all the while wondering where God is. Vicky remembers her recent conversation with Uncle Douglas and his explanation that God's ways are not always our ways.[15]

Vicky realizes that the rock slide and the possibility of death have made Zachary value his life again. She moves from a place of protesting disbelief to a place of faith. She ponders the mystery:

> "The point was that now I knew it didn't matter whether or not I understood. It didn't matter because even if I didn't understand, there was something there to *be understood*."[16]

Then Vicky is filled with calm and drifts off to sleep. Almost immediately she hears the shouts of the search party. They are found!

Madeleine L'Engle often writes about the mystery of faith —including the mystery of how individuals come to faith—but she never seeks to solve it. In her recent books, as well as in her workshops, she cites the phrase about God that means the most to her. It comes from the name Rudolf Otto gives God in his book *The Idea of the Holy*: "*mysterium tremendum et fascinans.*" This Latin phrase translates (albeit somewhat poorly) into English as "the tremendous and fascinating mystery."[17]

Something more of Madeleine's sense of the mystery of God is communicated in Grandfather Eaton's love of seventeenth-century poetry. Grandfather's reading of Henry Vaughan's poem "Night" to Vicky offers imagery that takes the heart where no pure intellect dares to tread:

> "There is in God, some say,
> A deep but dazzling darkness: as men here
> Say it is late and dusky, because they
> See not all clear.
>
> Oh for that Night, where I in him
> Might live invisible and dim!"[18]

Whenever Vicky Austin's grandfather appears as a key figure in one of Madeleine's novels, there is bound to be an abundance of religious references and deep spirituality. In *A Ring of Endless Light*, in which the Vaughan quotation appears, Grandfather Eaton is ill with leukemia. The entire Austin family has come to be with him at Seven Bay Island during what will be his last months of life.

The story begins with another man's funeral, that of Commander Rodney. During the funeral, Vicky thinks about life and death and God, and she remembers a time when Commander Rodney's son Leo was on a religious kick, telling Vicky he had all the answers about God. Grandfather had quietly reminded them of St. Augustine's words:

"If you think you understand, it isn't God."[19]

This is Madeleine's gentle way of reminding her readers yet again of her belief that, as finite human beings, we cannot understand God.

Later, as Vicky continues to reflect on the irreversible changes death brings, she remembers that Grandfather had once told her

> if someone kills a butterfly, it could cause an earthquake in a galaxy a trillion light-years away.[20]

This "butterfly effect" concept put forth by astrophysicists wonderfully conveys Madeleine's belief that everything that exists is interconnected—butterflies and daffodils, stars and galaxies. For her, everything belongs together in the fabric of the world God has created. She abhors the divisions that human beings and their institutions have created. She writes, for example, in *A Stone for a Pillow,* that it is a mistake to think God loves Christians better than people who profess other religious beliefs. Trusting that each of us is a child of God,[21] Madeleine believes that we are each called to be co-creators with God, according to our gifts and talents. For her, the artist's creative activity is almost identical to contemplative prayer—and a very humbling experience.

Madeleine gives us a further glimpse into her concept of prayer in *A Ring of Endless Light* when Vicky asks her grandfather how he prays for someone. He replies,

> "There are many different ways. I simply take him into my heart, and then put him into God's hand."[22]

This statement is a reflection of Madeleine's way of praying: She presents her deepest personal concerns to God and puts them into God's hands.

Madeleine's fantasy *An Acceptable Time* reveals further her belief in the possibility of having an intimate relationship with our

Source. The main character, Polly O'Keefe, has been sent to spend some time with her grandparents, Mr. and Mrs. Murry of *A Wrinkle in Time*.[23] Shortly after she arrives, Zachary Gray, the young man who pursued Vicky Austin in *The Moon by Night*, shows up. He had met Polly in Athens and then followed her to Cyprus the previous summer when she worked as a "gofer" at a writers' conference.

Polly and Zachary meet a family friend, Bishop Colubra.[24] He shares with them his discovery of a mysterious "window" through which people from the distant past can enter the present, and people from the present can go back into the past. Inadvertently Zachary and Polly enter the time warp window and end up in an adventure with people who lived in their same geographical location three thousand years earlier. Polly hears Anaral, a young woman from the ancient time, sing a song. When Polly asks her to explain the lyrics, Anaral replies,

> "The good-morning song to our Mother, who gives us the earth on which we live . . . teaches us to listen to the wind, to care for all that she gives us, food to grow . . . the animals to nurture, and ourselves. We ask her to help us to know ourselves, that we may know each other, and to forgive . . . to forgive ourselves when we do wrong, so that we may forgive others. To help us walk the path of love, and to protect us from all that would hurt us."[25]

Anaral's song is indicative of Madeleine's belief in a God who is above gender issues. She states that, in her earlier books, she called God "he" because this was the language she had been taught. but she is quick to affirm that she does not think of God in terms of gender.[26] Beginning with *And It Was Good*, the first book of the *Genesis Trilogy*, Madeleine refers to God as "El," the Hebrew word for "Lord." "El" sounds and acts like a pronoun, but in English it carries no gender weight.

Madeleine makes the point that personal pronouns are natural to use when describing a personal God, but when we decide that one pronoun—or one idea about the nature of God—is final, complete, without error, we run into trouble. Through Anaral's good-morning song to the Mother, Madeleine expresses, ever so gently, the idea that the God who has so often been thought of as Father might also be considered Mother.

This is not the first time Madeleine has affirmed her belief that, because God is above gender, it is as proper and important to consider the nurturing aspects of El. She is clear about her own need for the nurturing of a Mother God when she is feeling down:

> ... I need the mother to pull me onto her lap, hold the protective wings about me, rock me, tell me that it will be all right.[27]

As *An Acceptable Time* continues, Polly and Anaral discover that Bishop Colubra, believing Zachary and Polly to be in grave danger, has followed them into the past. They find him praying to Christ. Polly reminds the bishop that Christ has not yet been born in the time period to which they have been transported. The bishop reminds her that Christ is eternal:

> "The Second Person of the Trinity always was, always is, always will be, and I can listen to Christ now, three thousand years ago, as well as in my own time, though in my own time I have the added blessing of knowing that Christ, the alpha and omega, the source, visited this little planet. We are that much loved. But nowhere, at any time or in any place, are we deprived of the source."[28]

This section reveals Madeleine's belief that the Christ principle, the Logos, the Word, has always been part of the Godhead. She sees the Incarnation of God in Christ as a means of giving us a glimpse of the nature of God, and suggests that the best way to understand God with our finite minds is to "look at" Jesus the Christ:[29]

In the most glorious possible demonstration of God *in* and *part of* Creation, God came to us in Jesus of Nazareth, fully partici-pating in our human birth and life and death and offering us the glory of Easter.[30]

Through God-made-human, she believes, we have also been given a glimpse of humanity at its best:

The Incarnation hallows our human lives.[31]

And further, as she writes in *Sold into Egypt*:

Jesus came to us as a truly human being, to show us how to be human. . . . And God does not ask us to be perfect; God asks us to be human.[32]

The struggle to understand human nature—and God's na-ture—is a major theme in Madeleine L'Engle's fiction. In *An Ac-ceptable Time*, Polly and Klep, the wounded future leader of the People Across the Lake, discuss God and conclude that they do not believe in different Gods, but in the same God, whom they each see differently.[33]

For Madeleine, God is above all denominational and tradi-tional divisions. This may be one reason her work has been read by people of all religious beliefs for decades: Readers recognize that she speaks and writes about the Author of the Universe.

When pressed for a description of God, Madeleine responds that the only thing she can say for certain about God is that God is love.[34] She rejects any idea of God as an angry, condemning, Moses-in-a-bad-temper kind of God,[35] believing that a thorough examination of Scripture is clear about God's unqualified love.[36]

The theme of God as love emerges subtly in *An Acceptable Time*. Polly is taken hostage by the People Across the Lake because they think she is a healer who can bring them relief from the drought they are experiencing. In fact, it is Zachary who has betrayed Polly into the hands of the People Across the Lake, hoping to persuade their "healer" to fix Zachary's rheumatic heart as a reward. When he discovers the real danger into which his foolishness has thrust Polly, he rebels and is taken captive himself. Polly escapes but comes back to rescue Zachary.

Upon her return to the People Across the Lake, Polly hears the wind stirring, listens to the heart of the oak, and feels a sense of trust:

> Yes, she would trust. The universe is a *uni*verse. Everything is connected by the love of the Creator.[37]

And with this unqualified love comes forgiveness. There may be no clearer expression of Madeleine's idea about the grace of God than that found when Bishop Colubra, in *An Acceptable Time*, quotes William Langland:

> " 'And all the wickedness in the world that man might work or think is no more to the mercy of God than a live coal in the sea.' "[38]

The theme of God's mercy is developed even more fully in *A Live Coal in the Sea*, an intergenerational novel whose characters often stand in need of forgiveness, and whose title is taken directly from this Langland quotation. In fact, it seems more and more apparent in Madeleine's writing that the forgiveness of God is a concept she finds important to the expression of her own theology.

A Live Coal in the Sea also provides Madeleine with the opportunity to remind readers that science and religion are not enemies. Her protagonist, Camilla Dickinson, is an astronomer married to a minister. Throughout the book there are conversations between these two individuals that voice Madeleine's belief that the scientific view of the cosmos can only enrich our understanding of the Creator. As science reveals new information about the galaxies, Madeleine reminds us that it is only our *understanding* of God that might have to change, not God.[39] By breaking free of traditional, institutional teachings about God, Madeleine opens her belief not only to a God who is expansive, but also to a God with whom we can be angry, or doubt, or explore without fear.

An idea that persists in her writing is that God does not need our protection—especially not from scientific discovery—since God made everything.[40] In fact, Madeleine proposes that we should actively *disturb* the universe, even when it means questioning God. She makes a delightful and enlightening comment on this in A *Stone for a Pillow*:

> My faith in God, who is eternally loving and constant even as my understanding grows and changes, makes life not only worth living, but gives me the courage to dare to disturb the universe when that is what El calls me to do. Sometimes simply being open, refusing to settle for finite answers, disturbs the universe. Questions are disturbing, especially those which may threaten our traditions, our institutions, our security. But questions never threaten the living God, who is constantly calling us, and who affirms for us that love is stronger than hate, blessing stronger than cursing.[41]

Refusing to believe that her understanding could ever plumb the depths of God's nature, she remains open to new ways to think and talk about God. In *Sold into Egypt*, she speaks of the necessity of being open to changes in our thinking about God and to the possibility of new revelations from and about God.[42] Then, as our knowledge changes and grows, she suggests, our images and icons need to change or they become idols.

There seems to be a new development, or emphasis, in Madeleine's in her latest books, particularly *Bright Evening Star*. She reiterates her firm conviction that truth is different from, and not the same as, fact. She writes quite to the point about her belief that not only is grasping for power on the human plane a source of evil and pain, but that one of the most important characteristics of God is that El gives up power to "interfere" in human lives in order to teach us how to live and how to love. For her, this giving up of power characterizes the very essence of God's power:

> "God is lavish with power, not grasping it, as we do, but joyfully giving it away."[43]

The paradox, Madeleine observes, is that in spite of having given us free will, God "does not lose control of the divine plan."[44]

Bright Evening Star is perhaps the clearest, most specific statement of Madeleine's commitment to a God she believes created all that is and who loves the creation. If *A Wrinkle in Time* is, as Madeleine has said, her "love letter to God,"[45] *Bright Evening Star* may well be the Hallelujah Chorus of the *Messiah*.

CHAPTER IV
Light-Bearers

Jesus came to us as a truly human being,
to show us how to be human,
and we were so afraid of this humanness
that we crucified it, thinking it could be killed.
And today we are still afraid to be human,
struggling instead with a perfectionism
which is crippling, or which in some cases
can lead to a complete moral breakdown.
We are not perfect.[1]

At Madeleine L'Engle's invitation, I visited her at Crosswicks, her beloved home in Goshen, Connecticut. After her son, Bion, let me in, I immediately encountered Madeleine wearing a bathing suit, bearing a towel, and heading toward the indoor pool. I soon joined her for a swim, and we talked until she finished her laps.

After our swim, we dressed and took cups of hot tea up to the "tower," Madeleine's writing room over the garage. We talked and laughed until dinner, when Bion, the chief chef, and his wife,

Laurie, joined us. After holding hands for the blessing, the four of us ate on the porch by candlelight, enjoying a glass of wine and stimulating conversation.

The next day, after Madeleine's morning swim, we went for a walk, accompanied by her beautiful golden retrievers. The path led us to a large, flat volcanic rock formation near the house, the model for the "star-watching rock" Madeleine introduced in *Meet the Austins*.

At noon, Madeleine prepared lunch, which we ate together on the verandah, enjoying more good conversation until time for my departure. As I drove away, I realized I had been privileged to see Madeleine L'Engle "the celebrity" relaxing at home, "off duty" for a while. In her small town, she is regarded as an ordinary human being who just happens to be a well-known writer.

But the same Madeleine L'Engle who greeted me in her bathing suit and fixed my lunch receives hundreds of letters each week calling her a special person, raving about her gifts of inspiration, thanking her for the comfort her writing has brought, and asking for advice. Madeleine claims not to "know" the person addressed in these letters. The Madeleine she "knows" best is the one with whom I swam and walked at Crosswicks.

Of course, there is only one Madeleine L'Engle, a woman striving to keep her balance, to honor her private self in a world where public people are so revered. Circumstances in her life have helped her maintain her perspective: There have been bumps in the road. Madeleine knows about being physically imperfect: She has terrible eyesight, which makes everything appear a blur without her contact lenses; one leg is shorter than the other; at nearly six feet, she is taller than most women. She has experienced rejection and failure: The two-year period in which *A Wrinkle in Time* was repeatedly turned down by publishers hurt her deeply. Madeleine knows what it is like to be wounded and vulnerable.

Madeleine's acceptance of the full range of our humanity is evident in the chapter entitled "Bodies" in *Penguins and Golden*

Calves. Here she affirms the wonder and beauty of the human body designed and created by God and describes how our bodies can be icons pointing beyond ourselves to our Creator. In one of her most personal discussions of what it means to be human, to be "bodies," she describes the two times her husband, Hugh's, body was an icon for her—on their wedding night and at the time of his death:

> The human body, that which Jesus honoured in his own flesh, can be a beautiful icon of the love of God, the body in its entirety, the eyes, the fingers, the toenails, the body hair—every single part. Paul affirms that the lowliest parts of the body are as important as those we consider the more "honourable."[2]

In an ode to both the human body and the experience of aging, Madeleine concludes her chapter with these words:

> I have worn my body for nearly eighty years, and I am comfortable with it. I would, given the choice, have made myself a beauty, but it's probably a good thing I was not given a choice. My parents in other ways were generous with their genes. I am grateful for my goodly heritage. As I grow older, I want to continue to honour my body, to care for it, but not idolize it. I have been blessed with a husband who honoured my body, and with friends who love me just as I am, warts and all. We talk together around the dinner table and we wonder what has happened to escalate the warfare between men and women. And I think it is probably because we no longer see each other as icons, but as consumers.

> We need to see each other as sacred once more, because God has made us and what God has made is sacred.[3]

While Madeleine's views about human nature and human beings have been shaped by her personal experiences, other factors must also be considered. Any discussion of these matters must take into account her belief that Jesus came to earth to show human beings not only what God is like but also what humanity is like.

Madeleine is persuaded that the Incarnation dignifies humanity because, in the act of God taking on human form, the divine embraces the matter of which human beings are made.[4] She sees in Jesus the necessary interconnection of spirit and flesh, the touching of heaven and earth, and it leads to her conviction that humans are both spirit and flesh, and that to deny either of these aspects of ourselves is to deny our full potential and value.

Bright Evening Star is Madeleine's hymn to the mystery of both the incarnation and human-being-ness. She writes that the full humanness of Jesus brings with it lessons about who we are and who we are supposed to be, and she continues her theme of "giving up power":

> When God made creatures with free will, that was a tremendous giving away of controlling power.[5]

Here she goes one step further, declaring that our free will is a gift from God and expressing how this gift "cost" God:

> When we creatures were made with free will, the ability to make choices and decisions, God gave up control in a way so radical we have never quite understood it as we continue to strive for power. When God saw what a miserable mess we were making by clinging to power, Christ threw power away once again and came to us to show us that power was literally killing us.[6]

> Christ, the Second Person of the Trinity, the Maker of all the galaxies, gave up all power so that this power might instead be human, mortal, finite, and that we might understand that this very humanness, mortality, finiteness, if we would only accept it, would be made divine, immortal, and infinite by God in the fullness of time.[7]

Madeleine suggests that we can learn much about our humanness from Christ. For her, the idea that the Creator of the stars and galaxies became a human being is a lesson in humility. Madeleine underscores that, just as Jesus did not put himself in the center but always pointed beyond himself to God the Creator, so we, too, must never make the mistake of putting ourselves in the place of God. As she writes in *And It Was Good,* we are to be light-bearers, but we are not the Light.[8]

This belief also surfaces in *The Moon by Night.* The poems and Scripture passages Vicky Austin's grandfather had painted on the walls of the loft of his home demonstrate his humble understanding that he is not the Light:

> "I will lift up mine eyes unto the hills
> From whence cometh my help.
> My help cometh from the Lord
> Which made heaven and heart."[9]

Further, in *A Ring of Endless Light,* when Vicky describes her grandfather as being

> empty of all the horrid things, and filled with gentleness and strength,[10]

she quotes a poem by Thomas Brown that is also painted on Grandfather's wall. This verse points to the One beyond:

> "If thou could'st empty all thyself of self,
>   Like to a shell dishabited,
> Then might He find thee on the ocean shelf,
>   And say, 'This is not dead,'
>   And fill thee with Himself instead."[11]

For Madeleine, Jesus is the ultimate example of love because he loved and affirmed everyone he met, regardless of condition or status in society. Madeleine believes that we, too, are called to love, affirm, accept, forgive, minister—to "see Christ" in everyone. This parallels the concept of *ousia,* a Greek word having to do with the realness of things, that essential part of a person nothing can destroy, the Christ within.

When she wrote about her mother's atherosclerosis in *The Summer of the Great-grandmother*, Madeleine understood that her mother's essence, her *ousia*, was still there, even when her ailing mother was "not herself."[12] A *Wrinkle in Time* gives another example of *ousia* when Meg Murry finds the *real*, essential part of her brother Charles Wallace and saves him by loving that part, even when the rest of him is mean and nasty and under the control of the naked brain, called IT.[13]

Being able to love fully, Madeleine believes, means being able to see the unique value of every aspect of Creation, to recognize that every creature, regardless of size, is of inestimable value to God. For example, in *A Wind in the Door*—the second volume of Madeleine's time fantasy series—Meg, Calvin, the school principal Mr. Jenkins, and a cherubim named Proginoskes have become microscopic entities inside a mitochondrion in a cell of desperately ill Charles Wallace's body. To save him, they must persuade an even tinier creature, a farandola named Sporos, to "deepen," or root. The very existence of Charles Wallace depends on this infinitesimal creature.

Another vital part of love, for Madeleine, is the ability to see and accept ourselves and others for who we and they really are. In *The Weather of the Heart*, Madeleine wrote a poem to her husband, Hugh, titled "To a Long Loved Love: 7." It poignantly reveals her thoughts about what it might mean to *really* see someone for who they are—and what we miss when we do not:

> Because you're not what I would have you be
> I blind myself to who, in truth, you are.
> Seeking mirage where desert blooms, I mar
> Your you. Aaah, I would like to see
> Past all delusion to reality:
> Then would I see God's image in your face,
> His hand in yours, and in your eyes his grace.
> Because I'm not what I would have me be,
> I idolize Two who are not any place,
> Not you, not me, and so we never touch.

Reality would burn. I do not like it much.
And yet in you, in me, I find a trace
Of love which struggles to break through
The hidden lovely truth of me, of you.[14]

Love, for Madeleine, is more than a feeling. In its highest form, she believes that love calls us to action, that we have the freedom, and the necessity, to choose that action, and that we are ultimately responsible for the choices we make.

This point is vividly demonstrated in *A Wrinkle in Time* when Meg must decide whether to return to the planet Camazotz to save Charles Wallace, who remains in IT's hypnotic clutches. Meg, who has just recovered from the near death she experienced when her father "tessered" (transported) her, knows that *someone* has to tesser back to Camazotz to save her brother. She looks for someone else to do it, protests, then weeps at the dreadful thought of returning to the evil planet. But she concludes that only she knows Charles Wallace well enough to save him.[15]

In this scene Madeleine makes clear her belief that God is present in all our endeavors, but that we must make choices and bear the responsibility for our actions. We have the freedom to choose to do right or wrong. Failing to exercise our free will makes us less than human; misusing our freedom invites us into the dangerous waters of disobedience. Madeleine suggests that perhaps "sin" is actually making the wrong choices or misusing free choice, and it happens when we become separated from our Source. In *The Rock That Is Higher*, Madeleine writes that to describe Jesus as "sinless" is really to say that he was never separated from his Source.[16] She believes God never separates from us, but rather it is we who have trouble maintaining the connection.

Zachary Gray is one of Madeleine's best examples of someone who has separated himself from his Source. In *The Moon by Night*, he ridicules Vicky for believing in God. At the end of *An Acceptable Time*, however, he repents for having chosen to betray Polly O'Keefe. When Bishop Colubra reminds him that the mercy of

God is far greater than all the "wickedness in the world" human beings can do, Zachary discovers that God has not abandoned him.[17]

Madeleine rejects the idea that we have inherited "sin" in some genetic fashion from our ancestors. This is evident in *A Ring of Endless Light* when she exposes her readers to one of the great thinkers of our time, Elie Wiesel. During a dinnertime discussion about God's providence and human nature, Grandfather leaves the table and returns with Wiesel's book *Messengers of God.* From this book, he reads Wiesel's statement that Adam bequeathed to humanity his death, not his sin. Wiesel clearly believed that neither sin nor guilt can be transmitted.[18]

God does not ask us to be perfect, Madeleine concludes, but only to be who we are. In fact, she sees fallibility as one of humanity's glories. Madeleine states she has learned and grown more through her mistakes and failures than through her successes. Fallible people, she writes, are free to grow, to change, to become; they are not stuck in their ideas of perfection, afraid to change.[19]

In *A Wrinkle in Time,* Madeleine makes no attempt to hide Meg's greatest faults: anger, stubbornness, and impatience. In fact, these very "faults" are a necessary part of her saving Charles Wallace.[20] Once Meg reaches Camazotz, she experiences both anger and hatred in the presence of the naked brain, IT. The anger keeps her from falling immediately into IT's clutches. Her hatred helps her recognize IT's ability to hate. Her stubbornness keeps her standing there until she figures out how to save her brother—by understanding what she has that IT does not have. This is a classic portrayal of Madeleine's belief that not only do our fallibilities help break down our pride and arrogance, but that it is precisely out of our brokenness that we can serve God best.

The characters in Madeleine's more recent fiction, *A Live Coal in the Sea,* are real, flawed, and very human, which sets the stage for a book about sin, forgiveness, and grace. At the beginning of the book, the protagonist, Camilla Dickinson, has been asked by her college-age granddaughter to clear up a mystery about her parentage. As Camilla remembers the events of her life from her college days to the present, the reader re-experiences with her the choices, deeds, troubles, and mistakes made by several of the book's main characters. The story is intricately woven, right to its surprise ending, with the ever-present theme that where sin is present, forgiveness is needed; and that where forgiveness is needed, God's grace is present:

> And that's what it's all about: God's love. God's unmerited, unqualified love, waiting for us. We don't have to deserve that love which is ours, ours whether we want it or not. If we don't want it, that love can be terrible indeed. But if we reach out for God with love, God's love will surround us. God made us, made us in love, and that love will never falter.[21]

Perhaps one of Madeleine's most thought-provoking beliefs is that we are not as yet fully human:

> Jesus is us; and it's we who aren't us and haven't been, not since Adam and Eve.[22]

She sees each of us as being on an individual journey toward wholeness, toward becoming who we really are. And our best chance of growing into our full humanity, Madeleine observes, is to be connected with God, to nurture the connection with our Source.[23]

Among Madeleine's fictional characters who best exemplify wholeness, the ones who immediately come to mind are septuagenarians. The first is Grandfather Eaton of the Austin series. Grandfather is most clearly defined in *A Ring of Endless Light*, when he is dying of leukemia. As he faces his illness, he is filled with grace and courage; he is strong, yet unashamed to weep. As Madeleine portrays his wisdom, love of poetry, love of God, and love of family, she is laying out for her readers her idea of a whole human being.

Other models of wholeness include Katherine Vigneras and Felix Bodeway from *A Severed Wasp* and Bishop Colubra from *An*

Acceptable Time. Each of these individuals has lived long, suffered much, experienced loss and disappointment, and come to accept and love themselves. They have learned much about giving and receiving forgiveness, and are well on their way to becoming fully human.

But, as Madeleine points out in *And It Was Good,* becoming fully human does not happen in isolation. She explains this in the context of the two Creation stories in Genesis:

> The point is not which came first, the chicken or the egg, but that it is not good for the human being to be alone. Each of us needs others. Any single one of us, alone, cannot be the image of God; discovering that image within us is not a do-it-yourself activity. Before I can be an icon of the image of God, I must be with someone else, hand in hand.[24]

Madeleine is convinced that each of us is more whole when we are part of a larger community than when we are alone:

> We are most free when we are most willing to acknowledge our interdependence. Adam and Eve were free until they saw each other as separate and autonomous, and afraid of their Creator.[25]

Though all the men, women, and children who people the pages of Madeleine's books may be "companions" on the path toward fuller humanity, the specific community we call "family" takes on a particularly important role. The children in Madeleine's stories grow—not only into adulthood but into wholeness—through the love they experience in their families.

It should be noted that, although the fictional families Madeleine creates for her young characters are very traditional, she is quite aware of the different patterns "family" may take. In *The Rock That Is Higher,* she shares information about several family patterns she has experienced and writes that, there are dozens and dozens of ways to be a family. . . . Family tends to happen.[26]

Madeleine looks to Jesus' life, too, as a model for a community of love:

Jesus' family was a holy family. As all families are called on to be holy; with all our differences, opinionatedness, selfishness, we are redeemed by a love which is deeper than all our brokenness, a love given to us when the Maker of the Universe came to Mary's womb, to show incredible love for us all by becoming one of us. And so the holiness of all families was affirmed.[27]

Madeleine sees the differences among us, the wonderful uniqueness of each of us, as making a community more whole than one person alone can be. She illustrates this idea that *uniqueness* has more value than *sameness* in *A Wrinkle in Time*. On their first visit to Camazotz, Meg resists IT's spell by reciting first the multiplication table and then the Declaration of Independence. When she says the line about all men being created equal, she feels "IT seizing, squeezing her brain."[28] Through the hypnotized Charles Wallace, IT speaks:

"But that's exactly what we have on Camazotz. Complete equality. Everybody exactly alike."

For a moment her brain reeled with confusion. Then came a moment of blazing truth. "No! . . . *Like* and *equal* are not the same thing at all!"[29]

For Madeleine, this suggests that wholeness is not only an individual endeavor but a community process. She believes that, just as human beings are known, or "Named," by God, we are also called to Name other human beings. During her years in an English boarding school in Switzerland, Madeleine was known by the number 97, not a name. Later, she gave this hated experience to her teenage protagonist Philippa Hunter in *And Both Were Young.*[30] To this day, Madeleine is so opposed to being known by a number that she refuses to learn her Social Security number!

In several books, particularly *A Wind in the Door*, Madeleine proposes that our vocation as humans is to become Namers, to call others into being through understanding and love. The cherubim Proginoskes tells Meg that, since she has been assigned to him as a partner to accomplish three tests and to save Charles Wallace, she must be some sort of Namer. Meg asks Progo what it means to be a Namer. Since Progo has recently Named the stars, he says,

> "When I was memorizing the names of the stars, part of the purpose was to help them each to be more particularly the particular star each one was supposed to be. That's basically a Namer's job. Maybe you're supposed to make earthlings feel more human."[31]

Of all the pursuits to which Madeleine believes humans are called—to humility, to love, to choice, to wholeness, to Naming—perhaps the sum of it is simply that we are called to observe and contemplate the Creator and Creation and then to respond appropriately. Madeleine celebrates this in her 1985 Christmas letter as quoted in *Sold into Egypt*:

> Observe and contemplate.
> Make real. Bring to be.
> Because we note the falling tree
> The sound is truly heard.
> Look! The sunrise! Wait—
> It needs us to look, to see.
> To hear, and speak the Word.
>
> Observe and contemplate
> The cosmos and our little earth.
> Observing, we affirm the worth
> Of sun and stars and light unfurled.
> So let us, seeing, celebrate

The glory of God's incarnate birth
And sing its joy to all the world.

Observe and contemplate.
Make real. Affirm. Say Yes,
And in this season sing and bless
Wind, ice, snow; rabbit and bird;
Comet and quark; things small and great.
Oh, observe and joyfully confess
The birth of Love's most lovely Word.[32]

Along with modern scientists, Madeleine L'Engle believes that to observe something is to change it. The subtle—and amazing—underlying conclusion to this is that God *calls* humans to complete Creation by observing and contemplating it. Madeleine sees this as one way we can fulfill our purpose of becoming co-creators with God. In *Sold into Egypt* she writes,

> If we are responsible for the *being* of things, if we are, as this new theory implies, co-creators with God, this gives the sentient, questioning human being an enormous responsibility. Rather than swelling our egos, it should awaken in us an awed sense of vocation. We human creatures are called to be the eyes and ears and nose and mouth and fingers of this planet. We are called to observe all that is around us, to contemplate it, and to make it real.[33]

Madeleine goes on to point out that part of the "realness" of life, part of being human, is to be aware that we will die:

> To be a human being is to be born, to live, to die. We have a life span.[34]

Yet she is convinced that death is not the end of us. This emerges in *A Ring of Endless Light* when Vicky Austin has a serious conversation with Adam Eddington about death. A newborn dolphin at the marine biology lab where Adam works has died, and Adam tells Vicky that the wife and daughter of his boss, Jeb, were killed in an earlier car accident. Adam states his belief:

> "If we're still around after we die, it will be more like those mo-
> ments when we let go, than the way we are most of the time.
> It'll be—it'll be the self beyond the self we know."[35]

This concept of life beyond death fits with Madeleine's belief that being human is more a journey than a condition. In *Sold into Egypt,* which is based on the biblical story of Jacob's favorite son and his many-colored coat, Madeleine tells of Joseph being sold by his brothers and ending up a servant in Egypt. We also learn of his journey from being an arrogant, spoiled brat into servanthood and prison, and finally into high office:

> Joseph was forced to look low for the Creator, dumped into a
> pit, sold to strangers, sold again in Egypt, thrown into prison,
> catapulted into powers. And with each strange reversal he
> grew, grew into a human being. . . . To be a human being is to
> know clearly that anything good we do is sheer gift of grace,
> that God's image in us shines so brightly that its light is visi-
> ble.[36]

Madeleine portrays Joseph's transforming pilgrimage as a journey that brought him closer to his calling as a child of God and made him more fully human. Through his adventures and misad-ventures, Madeleine conveys her belief that we are always growing into "full and complex human being(s),"[37] even, or perhaps espe-cially, through hardship.

One of the loveliest passages dealing with this idea of growing into fullness appears in *A Wind in the Door.* The farandola Sporos must "deepen" if Charles Wallace's life is to be saved. When Mr. Jenkins asks what it means for Sporos to deepen, the cherubim Proginoskes explains,

> "When Sporos Deepens . . . it means he comes of age. It
> means he grows up. The temptation for farandola or for man

or for star is to stay an immature pleasure-seeker. When we seek our own pleasure as the ultimate good we place ourselves as the center of the universe. A fara or a man or a star has his place in the universe, but nothing created is the center."[38]

In the stories of Joseph and Sporos, Madeleine L'Engle underscores her conviction that for humans to find wholeness and freedom they must be rooted in God. Only then can their spirits "sing with the stars" and "dance with the galaxies."[39]

CHAPTER V

The Family Table

When we gathered around the table,
with the candles lit under the hurricane globes,
we all held hands and sang grace.
I wondered how Adam would feel,
but I looked down at the table and not across at him.
And then I heard his voice,
and he was singing with John, in a good, strong baritone.[1]

At the root of Madeleine L'Engle's interest in families lie her lonely childhood years. Madeleine's mother was in her late thirties when Madeleine, her only child, was born after many years of marriage and several miscarriages. Shortly after Madeleine's birth, her father returned from World War I with mustard-gas-damaged lungs that required him to give up his work as a war correspondent. He settled into a life of writing late into the night and sleeping well into the morning. The combination of the poor health of both of Madeleine's parents, along with their desire to continue traveling together as they had done before Madeleine's birth, increased their daughter's loneliness.

In *The Rock That Is Higher*, as well as in other books, Madeleine has written forcefully about the painful experiences of her New York City childhood. Because she did not do well in school, her teachers assumed she was not smart. At home she spent a great deal of time alone in her room where she read profusely. In addition, she kept a journal and, by the age of five, had written her first story.

This brilliant but lonely little girl was already seeking answers to the puzzles of human existence, without being consciously aware of the cosmic nature of her inquiries.[2] While painful, that same isolated childhood provided the seed for her rich intuitive sense and her creative writing talent.

Given her "only child" status, it is not surprising that Madeleine L'Engle has created several large, more or less traditional, fictional families, the most prominent being the Murrys, the Austins, and the Davidsons.[3] Many of the activities and values of these families resemble those of the "real life" family that Madeleine and her husband, Hugh Franklin, built with their children. The experiences of the protagonists in these fictional families provide clues about Madeleine's family values, which are confirmed in her autobiographical and nonfiction books.

It is interesting to note that the Murrys, Austins, and Davidsons are all two-parent families. Also, while the mothers are well-educated and involved in professional activities, their work does not take them away from their homes. Mrs. Murry, who has two Ph.D. degrees, does her research "full-time" in a home laboratory off the kitchen. Mrs. Austin is a professional musician who has chosen to set aside her career to be a full-time wife and mother.[4]

These characters reflect some of Madeleine's own struggles between pursuing her career and being a mother. Before she married, *The Small Rain* and *18 Washington Square, South* had been published, and *Ilsa* was about to be. In the earliest years of her marriage, both she and Hugh had careers. Although Hugh shared the housework and child care, Madeleine, because she wrote at home and was not traveling much at that time, experienced the larger share of the frustration caused by juggling the needs of her young children with the emerging demands of her career. She writes about the joys and sorrows of what she calls "the precarious triangle of wife-mother-writer"[5] in *A Circle of Quiet*, her first autobiographical book.

The fictional families Madeleine L'Engle has "birthed"—including children, adults, even pets—have taken on lives of their own, sometimes even growing and changing while they are "off stage" waiting for their next appearance in another of her books.[6] Madeleine admits freely in *The Rock That Is Higher* that

> the characters of my stories *are* family for me, and that is why many of them appear in more than one book. I don't want to leave them at the end of a book. I want to find out what happens to them.[7]

Madeleine focuses on families where there is love, joy, and hopefulness. She does, however, occasionally portray children from families where these qualities are lacking. Calvin O'Keefe, for example, is an often-ignored member of a large, poor family. His mother does not hesitate to beat the children and she does not keep her house clean. Another character, Zachary Gray, has been given much in the way of material possessions, yet little in the way of intimacy and love.

Because of the fame of the widely read *A Wrinkle in Time*, the Murry family is perhaps the best known of Madeleine's families (see the diagram on page 180). There are four children: Meg, the oldest; Sandy and Dennys, the twins; and Charles Wallace, the youngest. Both parents hold Ph.D. degrees in science. The family also includes a large, nondescript dog named Fortinbras and a kitten, and they all live in an old farmhouse in New England. The members of the Murry family clearly love one another and take obvious joy in each other. A vivid example of this occurs at the end of *A Wrinkle in Time* when Mr. Murry returns home, after about a year's absence, with Meg, Charles Wallace, and Calvin O'Keefe, who have gone to rescue him. Their journey ends in the twins' vegetable garden.

> Mr. Murry was running across the lawn, Mrs. Murry running toward him, and they were in each other's arms, and then there was a tremendous happy jumble of arms and legs and hugging, the older Murrys and Meg and Charles Wallace and the twins, and Calvin grinning by them until Meg reached out and pulled him in and Mrs. Murry gave him a special hug all of his own. They were talking and laughing all at once, when they were startled by a crash, and Fortinbras, who could bear being left out of the happiness not one second longer, cata-pulted his sleek black body right through the screened door to the kitchen. He dashed across the lawn to join in the joy, and almost knocked them all over with the exuberance of his greeting.[8]

While more readers may know the Murry family, it is the Austin family (see the diagram on page 181) that reveals more completely Madeleine's view of family life. Reading the Austin series—*Meet the Austins, The Moon by Night,* and *A Ring of Endless Light*—is like stepping into a warm, bright room filled with people who, like the members of the Murry family, love each other and enjoy being together.[9] The father is a physician, and Mrs. Austin, who once sang professionally, is a full-time wife and mother. There are four Austin children: John is the oldest; Vicky, the narrator and protagonist of the stories, is second; Suzy comes next; and Rob is the youngest. Other characters include Dr. Austin's younger brother, Uncle Douglas; Mrs. Austin's father, Grandfather Eaton; Maggy, an orphaned child who comes to stay with them for a brief time; Zachary Gray, a friend who enters the picture in the second and third books of the trilogy; and the family's two dogs, Mr. Roch-ester the Great Dane and Collette the French poodle.

Regarding pets as part of the family is typical of Madeleine, for whom pets are important. The Franklins always had pets, from Madeleine's beloved golden retriever, Tino, who kept her company when she was not traveling, to Tatiana, her little white cat who awaits her when she comes home.

In the Austin family everyone has chores to do and a role to play. For example, each child has assigned tasks related to dinner preparation: John is responsible for heavy things such as leaves for the table, Vicky sets out the china, Suzy adds the silverware, and Rob arranges napkins and table mats. At dinnertime, everyone holds hands around the table for grace—a ritual that was also a regular part of mealtime in the Franklin household. After supper at the Austins', everyone helps with the cleanup. Dr. Austin encourages the children:

> "If we all pitch in and do the dishes, we'll have time for some singing. Go get your guitar, Victoria, and the kids and I'll take the dishes to the kitchen."[10]

On most evenings, Mrs. Austin plays the piano or guitar, and the others gather around and sing. When the children go to bed, Mother reads aloud, and both parents pray with the children. These scenes also mirror Madeleine and Hugh's patterns: They, too, read to their children nightly and said prayers with them.[11]

As *Meet the Austins* opens, the family is waiting for "Daddy" to come home from work. Vicky describes it as a "nice, normal, noisy evening."[12] While supper is being prepared, classical music is playing on the radio/phonograph. This nice, normal, noisy evening is interrupted by a phone call announcing the death of a close family friend whom the children call "Uncle Hal." That night at bedtime, Mother reads to the children, tucks them in, and after lights are out, says evening prayers with them, as usual. But this night she does not sing to them.

As the Austins come to terms with Uncle Hal's death, Madeleine uses the story to emphasize her belief that part of a family's responsibility is to be present with loved ones when death comes. This echoes Madeleine's experience after her mother died. Her friend

Canon West came to Crosswicks for what Madeleine called a "house mass." In *The Summer of the Great-grandmother*, she wrote of this family event that included dogs and babies wandering around, and gathered family members representing "Congregational, Roman Catholic, Jewish, agnostic, Anglican, atheist"[13] views:

> This time out of time in the absolute familiarity of the living room is healing and redemptive for me. . . . Canon West had us sit around the living room as we usually do for our home services. . . . And there in the living room is, for me, the Church.[14]

In *Two-Part Invention*, her book about both the early years and the last months of her marriage, Madeleine also describes the entire family being present, this time because Hugh was terribly sick. This theme of "being present" to each other runs through other books as well. In *A Ring of Endless Light*, the Austins stay with Grandfather Eaton during his last months of life. In *Certain Women*, David Wheaton's daughter, Emma, and his wife, Alice, stay with him during his last weeks of life on a "shabbily comfortable"[15] fifty-foot boat called the *Portia*, and other family members visit. These scenes make a consistent statement about Madeleine's conviction that dying is a family affair not to be experienced alone.

The Austin family faces a radical change with Uncle Hal's death: An unhappy ten-year-old orphan named Maggy comes to live with them. Maggy's father was killed in the same crash that took Hal's life. Since Maggy's mother died earlier, Uncle Hal's wife, Aunt Elena, had been given temporary custody. However, because of her demanding schedule as a concert pianist, Aunt Elena asks the Austins if they would keep Maggy for a while.

On the evening that Maggy arrives—and after the younger children are asleep—Mother takes Vicky and John to Hawk Mountain to look at the stars and talk. The visit to Hawk Mountain seems to be a family ritual, similar to Madeleine's practice of taking her children to the "star-watching rock" at Crosswicks to talk.

On the mountain, Vicky and John and their mother talk over their feelings about Uncle Hal's death and Maggy's upsetting arrival.[16] This is how Vicky describes the experience:

> "We sat there, close, close, and it was as though we could feel the love we had for one another moving through our bodies as we sat there together, moving from me through Mother, from Mother to John, and back again. I could feel the love filling me, love for Mother and John, and for Daddy and Suzy and Rob, too. And I prayed, 'Oh, God, keep us together, please keep us together, please keep us safe and well and together.' "[17]

John asks his mother why people have to die, why things have to change, why things cannot stay exactly the way they are. Mother replies,

> "We can't stop on the road of Time. We have to keep on going. And growing up is all part of it, the exciting and wonderful business of being alive. We can't understand it, any of us, any more than we can understand why Uncle Hal and Maggy's father had to die. But being alive is a gift, the most wonderful and exciting gift in the world. And there'll undoubtedly be many other moments when you'll feel this same way, John, when you're grown up and have children of your own."[18]

Feeling much better, they return home and stand outside looking up at the stars, appreciating the night. Dr. Austin, just coming home after visiting a patient, joins them. As he stands with his arm around his wife, Vicky notes that

> it was so beautiful that for the moment the beauty was all that mattered; it wasn't important that there were things we never would understand.[19]

Other family concerns emerge as the Austin story progresses. The children's struggle to come to terms with "good and evil," for example, is illustrated when Vicky's younger sister, Suzy, takes it upon herself to become a vegetarian. Suzy, a compassionate girl who wants to be a doctor, is concerned about eating meat from animals, and family discussions ensue about the problems related to a diet that includes meat. John reminds them that Grandfather Eaton believes that choices are not always between evil and good, but that we sometimes have to choose between two evils or two goods.

Eventually, Suzy becomes so hungry from her self-made vegetarian diet that she takes some candy from a store without paying for it. When her parents find out, Suzy at first lies about the incident. They confront her, stressing the importance of not deceiving them, and then instruct her to apologize.[20] The firm but gentle way Dr. and Mrs. Austin handle this touchy situation serves as a lesson from Madeleine on good parenting.

Not all of the Austin encounters are serious. Just as practical jokes were common in the Franklin household, the Austins have fun together when they play a colossal joke on Uncle Douglas. Douglas has urged the family to be on especially good behavior when he brings a girlfriend to visit. This is all the invitation the family needs. They decide to pretend to be a snobby family, and they dress up in an unsightly assortment of old clothes and costumes. Daddy plays the role of "Grooves" the butler, and Aunt Elena plays the role of "Olga" the maid. The "girlfriend" turns out to be a distant cousin of Maggy's who is checking out the Austin family to see if they are worthy of caring for Maggy. They pass![21]

Just as Madeleine's own children read and were read to, so are the Austin children: Books such as *The Secret Garden, Dr. Doolittle,* and *The Sword in the Stone* are Austin children favorites. The adults of the Austin family are readers, too: Grandfather Eaton, a book lover at heart, has made the horse stalls in his converted-stable home into bookcases and bookshelves. During conversations at mealtime, it is not uncommon for Grandfather to jump up from the table to get one of his beloved books and read a paragraph to make a point.[22] We learn that Mrs. Austin is reading *Anna Karenina*. The mention of this and other fine books reflects the value Madeleine places on the art of reading and affirms her love of good books, poetry, and music.

Many other Austin family experiences reflect those of the Franklins' family life, including the importance of rituals for special dates and days, especially Thanksgiving and Christmas. In *The Moon by Night*, Zachary takes Vicky to see the play *The Diary of Anne Frank*. The Franks' celebration of Hanukkah reminds Vicky of Christmas at Thornhill, the New England village in which she has spent her life:

> Every Christmas Eve in Thornhill we have a special candlelight service, and Mother always sings the solo part of *Lullay My Liking* and when we get home there are certain carols we always sing and Daddy reads *The Night before Christmas* and *St. Luke* while we hang up our stockings. Well, the Hanukkah festival has traditions like that, candles in an eight-branched candelabra, and as part of the ritual the mother of the family says, "I will lift up mine eyes unto the hills," and everybody is full of joy and peace. Just the way we always are at Christmastime.[23]

The Austins' ten-week camping trip described in *The Moon by Night* exemplifies Madeleine's appreciation of family unity. There is nothing better than the close quarters of a camping trip for creating togetherness—as well as for activating irritation—among family members, and the Austins' trip is no exception. Early in the vacation, Vicky complains that she is tired of all the togetherness they are having. Later, Suzy reprimands her for this, saying she has hurt their parents and asking why she made "that crack." When Vicky asks, "What crack?," Suzy replies,

> "About Togetherness. Jeepers, Vicky! We've never gone on about Togetherness. Because we *are* together. We don't have to make a *Thing* about it. We just *are*, and we always *will* be, just the way Mother and Grandfather are, even if they don't see each other for months and months and months, and the way we are about Uncle Douglas and all."[24]

Family togetherness at the dinner table takes on a special role in Madeleine L'Engle's books, perhaps in response to her childhood experience: Mr. and Mrs. Camp would dress every evening and make a special event of their dinner hour, but Madeleine was rarely included. She was often left to eat supper alone in her room. In *The Summer of the Great-grandmother*, Madeleine writes that, until her father's damaged lungs took the Camps abroad when she was twelve,

> I don't think I ever ate at the table with my parents except on Sunday, and then, Mother said, "You didn't know what to say to us." I preferred eating alone off a tray, with a book propped on my lap. This may explain why the entire family eating together, around the table, is so important to me.[25]

In *Sold into Egypt*, Madeleine describes the mealtime pattern that she and Hugh established with their children:

> The evening meal, the table set with the best china and crystal, and lit by candles, has always been sacramental for me, the focal point of the day. It is when the family gathers together, shares the day's events, and God's bounty. When our children were little I did not mind *when* we ate as long as we ate together. If Hugh was previewing a Broadway play we sometimes ate at five o'clock. If someone had an after-school project we ate at eight or eight thirty. The family dinner table is no longer tradition in many families today; it is a great loss.[26]

The dinner table scenes in much of Madeleine's fiction affirm her conviction of the importance of families gathering for meals. She considers family meals a time for

> gathering together, the time when meaning is made clear—the value and validity of our lives. There have been times of trouble when the dinner table has been the only affirmation available.[27]

At the table, Madeleine's characters informally discuss the day's events, literature, and music. They speak openly with each other in true conversation in which all family members are heard as equally valuable.

One of my favorite Austin family mealtime scenes occurs in *A Ring of Endless Light* when John brings Adam Eddington, his co-worker for the summer at the marine biology lab, home for supper. There is the usual holding of hands, singing of grace, and lighting of candles. Vicky wonders if they are really

> as peculiar a family as Zachary thought. On the other hand, I didn't think Zachary and his family were that average, either. Our family is our family and I've always taken us completely for granted, and I was glad Adam seemed to take us for granted, too, us kids and our parents, and our grandfather, who talked about gravity and levity and heaven and all the things Zachary said nobody talked about.[28]

For Madeleine, the evening meal is ultimately a reminder of the Eucharist, one of the most important sacraments of the Christian church. In *The Irrational Season,* she writes,

> Bread. Wine. A dinner table. The firm clasp of hands as we say grace. The warm flame of candles. It is all an affirmation of incarnation, of being, versus non-being.[29]

Perhaps Madeleine's views are best summarized in the following poem:

> Come, let us gather round the table.
> Light the candles. Steward, pour the wine.
> It's dark outside. . . . The taste of brine
> warm from fresh tears, is in the glass. Choosy
> guests will not come here. The bread is body
> broken. The wine is dark with blood. I'm doubting
> if half of those invited will turn up.
> Most will prefer to choose a different table,
> will go elsewhere with gentler foods to sup.
> And yet this is indeed a wedding feast

and we rejoice to share the bitter cup,
the crumbs of bread. For O my Lord, not least
of all that makes us raise the glass, is that we toast
You, who assembled this uncomely group:
our one mysterious host.[30]

One of the keys to Madeleine's outlook is that she chooses, in the midst of a world filled with pain, disappointment, and rejection, to live her life with the belief that the ultimate power behind everything is love and that this loving power, which Madeleine calls God, cares for each of us individually. This premise is clearly reflected in the Austin family stories—where the parents love each other and their children—and in Madeleine's own family. Asked what is the best thing she and Hugh did for their children, Madeleine responds, "We loved each other."[31]

For Madeleine, this love is not limited to the immediate, biological family. The Austin family is far more than a nuclear, traditional family of mother, father, and children. It is an extended family with close ties to uncles and grandparents, and arms open wide to visitors. This openness to extended family reflects the four-generational summers Madeleine experienced for decades at Crosswicks.

In *A Severed Wasp*, Madeleine introduces another extended family, the Davidsons (see the diagram on page 183), which has at its center a father who is dean of the Cathedral of St. John the Divine, a mother who is a physician, and four children. (Mrs./Dr. Davidson is Suzy Austin, grown up and married to Josiah Davidson from *The Young Unicorns*.) The Davidsons' story also includes people who do not fit into traditional family patterns, including divorced, remarried, single, and widowed individuals. For example, Felix Bodeway, retired bishop of the Cathedral, has divorced and never remarried. One of the nuns at the nearby Episcopal convent is the ex-wife of the current bishop. Mimi Oppenheimer, an orthopedic surgeon in her forties who has never married, is a happy, well-adjusted, single person who has found her family with friends.

As with Madeleine's other fictional families, the Davidsons are an extension of the author's own life situations. She knows many divorced, widowed, and single people who have found ways to make families that include a wide variety of children, parents, friends, and pets, and she has recreated family for herself.

In particular, after Hugh's death, Madeleine grew much closer to her grandchildren. When she first returned to her New York apartment, Madeleine's seventeen-year-old granddaughter, Charlotte Jones, and one of Charlotte's friends, Alysa, came to share the apartment. Charlotte's older sister, Léna, who was attending Barnard College, came and went as her schedule allowed. Madeleine tells stories of the intergenerational dinner parties they held, involving guests of all ages from infant to septuagenarian, including the young women's friends and Madeleine's. Madeleine cooked the meals, and the teenagers cleaned up. Dinner was shared around a large table, and hands were held for the blessing. Everyone participated in the stimulating conversation, and sometimes after dinner those who wished shared a poem or played the piano or some other musical instrument—scenes not unlike the Austin family dinners.

In addition to opening her home to her grandchildren, Madeleine has opened her arms to embrace a large group of men and women whom she calls her "godchildren." These are people she has met through correspondence, at workshops and conferences, and at speaking engagements across the country. She gives support in their times of need, as they do for her.

The strength of this "family" was evident after Madeleine's serious automobile accident in California in July 1991, which she describes in *The Rock That Is Higher*. Telephone calls went out over a network of friends, conveying the news and requests for prayer. Several of Madeleine's closest friends immediately rearranged plans so they could go to her bedside.

During the decade of her seventies, the families Madeleine has created are less traditional than the Murrys, Austins, O'Keefes, and Davidsons of her earlier years—perhaps because of a different Madeleine, a different market, and a society more open about the problems in intimate relationships. Madeleine has created two new families in more recent writing. The David Wheaton family of *Certain Women* is perhaps her most nontraditional family (see the diagram on page 182). Because the life of the patriarch of this family, David Wheaton, is a contemporary parallel to the life of the biblical King David, Madeleine portrays David Wheaton as having been married many times and having fathered many, many children. Madeleine uses this story as a reminder that marriage is not about either perfect relationships or perfect people, but about commitment, understanding, and above all, grace and forgiveness.

In *A Live Coal in the Sea* Madeleine introduces readers to the Xanthakos family (see the diagram on page 183), which has secrets and scars. She deals boldly with such topics as marital infidelity and homosexuality. This sets the stage for her reminder that, in families and in marriages that are rooted in love, when we hurt each other, we must also forgive each other—and that God's grace shows us the way.

As Camilla tells her granddaughter, Raffi, about her past, we learn about the close relationship that Camilla's husband's parents had. Camilla describes her first visit to her future husband's home, on the eve of their engagement, when she wondered,

> "How had they managed, Mac's parents, to get to the place of radiance in which they lived?"[32]

When Camilla told Olivia, Mac's mother, that she sensed this peace, this serenity, and she hoped she and Mac would have it, Olivia replied,

> "My dear, it does not come free, or without leaving scars. When china is broken, no matter how well it's mended, you can still see the crack . . . When I think of Art and myself, I know that our patches and glued-together cracks are visible, but they've held."[33]

At another point in the story, Raffi and her therapist, Louisa Rowan (Camilla's childhood friend), are conversing about the difficulty of creating and maintaining healthy friendships and relationships. When Louisa tells Raffi that the hard work is worth it, Raffi asks why. Louisa answers,

> "When two people, lovers, or sometimes friends, have an enduring care for each other, allow each other to be human, faulted, flawed, but real, then being human becomes a glorious thing to be. If the human race ever makes progress, that is how."[34]

In writing books such as *A Live Coal in the Sea*, where adults hurt each other by being unfaithful in marriage, brutal, or violent in their actions, Madeleine risks—and has received—criticism. Yet this is an outgrowth of her conviction that, by making the idea of a "perfect family" into an idol, we have fallen prey to the practice of idolatry. In *Penguins and Golden Calves: Icons and Idols*, Madeleine proposes in her chapter "Family Values" that there is no such thing as a "functional family; there certainly were no truly functional families in Scripture!"[35] Reminding readers of her lonely childhood, she suggests seeing families as icons, or "windows to God,"[36] instead of idols.

For Madeleine, even the imperfect parent-child relationship can be perceived as an icon revealing of God. In *Mothers and Daughters*, she writes:

> It would be wonderful, O Holy One,
> if we mothers and daughters were always perfect:
>
> "If I never raised my voice in annoyance—"
> "If I never snapped back."
> "If I didn't have to remind you at least twice a day—"
> "If I could remember to hang up my clothes."
> "If I realized, all the time, how precious you are to me—"
> "If I never forgot you're a pretty good mother,
>   most of the time."

But we're not perfect.
Just a human mother and daughter.
Help us to make the best of us, Lord.[37]

In recent years, Madeleine has paid increasing attention to friendship as an important aspect of relationships. Her friendship of over a quarter of a century with Luci Shaw has led to the publication of two books with Luci, trips together, and shared podiums at conferences. *Friends for the Journey*, which they co-authored, provides a vehicle for Madeleine to share her ideas about friendship. In the preface to this book of stories, poems, recipes, conversations, and essays, Madeleine and Luci write of their friendship that,

> close and warm as it is, ours has never been an exclusive friendship. It is based on *Hesed*, the evocative Hebrew word that means loving-kindness, reaching-out compassion, grace.[38]

One aspect of intimate friendship particularly important to Madeleine is what she calls "mutual solitude"—the ability to be together without having to speak.[39]

Madeleine reinforces her commitment to extended family in chapter ten of *Bright Evening Star* where she reminds us that Jesus had relationships with many persons beyond his own family. She also writes of her own experience:

> Are we limiting our thoughts? Mother, father, two or three children? Weren't Mary, Martha, and Lazarus a family? In my young to middle years, I was part of what is considered a traditional family, wife, husband, three children. For a while after my husband died, my family was my two college-age granddaughters: Charlotte lived with me for seven wonderful years, and Léna was in and out. Now it is Bara, my apartment mate, who stays with me two or three nights a week. My family is my prayer group, my writers' workshops. It is my children and grandchildren and godchildren. What is family?[40]

The core of Madeleine's answer to the question, "What is family?" lies in a simple response: When we treat each other like family, we are family.[41] From my own experience, as a single woman sharing her home with a divorced mother of four and grandmother of eight, I especially appreciate Madeleine's definition of family as the people we are committed to, the people we treat with love and respect, and eat our meals with.[42] Also, the people we forgive.

This recognition of our need for forgiveness leads to what is perhaps the crux of "family" for Madeleine: we all—nuclear or extended families, traditional or nontraditional families—have a responsibility to each other, and especially to children. Although Madeleine chafes at being identified exclusively as a children's writer, over the years she has honored the responsibilities to children that have come with the fame of her award-winning fantasy *A Wrinkle in Time*. She receives hundreds of letters every year from children who are reading her books. By now, even the children of the children who first read *A Wrinkle in Time* are reading the book and writing to her. Out of her sense of responsibility to children, Madeleine faithfully answers these letters.[43] In *A Circle of Quiet*, she describes something of this commitment:

> So the challenge I face with children is the redemption of adulthood. We must make it evident that maturity is the fulfillment of childhood and adolescence, not a diminishing; that it is an affirmation of life, not a denial; that it is entering fully into our essential selves.[44]

For almost four decades, Madeleine's fictional families have provided young readers with models of healthy family systems. The impact these models may have had on tens of thousands of children is considerable. Perhaps one reason children respond so remarkably to Madeleine and her books is that she crafts her stories for them with immense care. She does not think writing for children is "easier" than writing for adults.

Children love Madeleine L'Engle. Wherever she goes to

speak, they gather around her as if she were the Pied Piper. I witnessed this at Kanuga, an Episcopal conference center in the mountains of North Carolina, where Madeleine was lecturing on "The Faces of God." During the five-day conference, Thursday was set aside as a special day for a picnic lunch so Madeleine could meet with the scores of children who had come with their families.

One evening, as we were walking toward the dining hall, I had an especially wonderful glimpse of Madeleine's "Pied Piper" effect on children. About six children of various ages ran up to us and surrounded Madeleine. She stopped to talk with them, and they fell over each other in their eagerness to tell her how much her books meant to them.

"I've read *A Wrinkle in Time* three times," said one.

Another told Madeleine that *A Ring of Endless Light* was her favorite.

A third admirer told Madeleine, "I have read every one of your books."

I was touched as I watched these children adoringly look up at Madeleine (all six feet of her!). She carefully addressed each child individually before moving on to dinner.

A similar display of mutual admiration occurred at a book signing. Although many adults came for autographs, the children dominated. As each child approached, Madeleine took a book, looked into the child's wonder-struck eyes, asked his or her name, answered a question or listened to some compliment, and enveloped the child with her smile. During hours of signing, she treated each child individually and warmly. Her manner was a benediction.

Children respond to and understand Madeleine's stories so immediately because they are still unselfconsciously in touch with their imaginations and open to their intuition. It is this "child" in each of us, regardless of our age, that Madeleine's families affirm, include, and value. In *A Circle of Quiet*, Madeleine writes,

Our responsibility to [children] is not to pretend that if we don't look, evil will go away, but to give them weapons against it. . . . Laughter, a gift for fun, a sense of play.[45]

This may well be the ultimate gift of Madeleine L'Engle's books, to children and adults alike: "weapons" of imagination and faith reflecting the Light against the darkness.

CHAPTER VI
Sacred Community

*We need to remember that the house of God
is not limited to a building
that we usually visit for only a few hours on Sunday.
The house of God is not a safe place.
It is a cross where time and eternity meet,
and where we are—or should be—challenged
to live more vulnerably, more interdependently.
Where, even with the light
streaming in rainbow colours through the windows,
we can listen to the stars.*[1]

When Madeleine L'Engle is in New York, which is most of the year, she spends the better part of each weekday at the library of the Cathedral of St. John the Divine serving as volunteer librarian. The library is a musty, dusty room filled with ancient and new books, a fireplace, desks, and tables. Here, with an assistant and her computer, Madeleine writes, takes phone calls, and meets with visitors . . . usually with a favorite dog sleeping nearby.

My visits with Madeleine at the Cathedral helped me gain a clearer picture of the church's importance to her. Her relationship with the church began in her New York childhood: Her Episcopalian parents taught her about a God who loved her unconditionally, and they took her to church. But Madeleine's early relationship with the church was a stormy one, and she has written about her lifelong efforts to unlearn and overcome the strict virtues she was taught. Her strict Anglican upbringing, combined with the stiff-upper-lip syndrome she experienced in the Anglican boarding school she attended as a teenager, taught her that any show of emotion was "bad form," that "tears, from either the male or the female of the species, are to be repressed."[2]

In retrospect, Madeleine realizes that her split with the church widened when her father died during her last year of high school at Ashley Hall. Neither the church nor the Anglican virtues she had learned so well helped her grieve or encouraged her grieving process. In *The Irrational Season,* she reflects that, by the time she started college, she "was through with the organized religious establishment" that had not been supportive in her time of grief.[3]

During her sophomore year at Smith College, Madeleine experienced a depression that she believes was directly related to unresolved grief over her father's death. It was not until she experienced the joys and heartbreak of being in love that she was able to weep freely over the death of her beloved father—and become free of the obsessive fear of death she had developed.[4]

Although Madeleine had left the Episcopal church of her childhood and opted for the life of the intellectual, she still longed for God.[5] After college, when she was writing and acting in New York, she often slipped into a pew at Ascension Episcopal Church on the corner of Tenth Street and Fifth Avenue on her way home from the theatre. She went not so much to pray as to "*be.*"[6] But it would be quite a while before she "officially" returned to any institutional church.

The same was true for her husband, Hugh Franklin, who had

left his Baptist institution. Madeleine wrote that, while never really leaving God, "We rebelled, each of us, against our particular religious establishment."[7] Their return to the church was inhibited by the then-current teachings of both Episcopalians and Baptists that prevented her and Hugh from taking communion in each other's denominational church.

It was the "community of marriage, of our growing family, a family of open doors"[8] that brought Madeleine her first conscious awareness of her need for the community and support a church could provide. Growing up as an only child, she had not experienced any sustained sense of community within her family; nor had the Anglican boarding school atmosphere been conducive to the building of a support system, religious or otherwise. Although Ashley Hall offered some sense of being part of something larger than herself, Madeleine's first sense of community outside the strictures of a church-related institution occurred with her college friends and, later, with people in the theatre.

Then in 1951, shortly after their first child was born, the Franklins moved to Connecticut and joined the small Congregational Church in Goshen. It was there that Madeleine "first experienced a truly Christian community."[9] The church became the center of their lives during this Crosswicks period. They found great friends, Madeleine served as choir director, and the Franklins became an integral part of a supportive community, the depth of which is indicated by an event that occurred some twenty-five years later. In January 1985, Madeleine and Hugh had returned from New York to spend some time at Crosswicks, and Madeleine slipped on the ice, breaking her shoulder. She discovered that her old support group from the Congregational Church was still there, ready to help.

As deep as those community bonds went, however, participating in the activities and less formal worship of the Congregational Church never fully satisfied Madeleine's need for the ritual of the liturgy. When the Franklins moved back to New York in

1960, Madeleine found that her spirit was fed in the liturgy of the Anglican Cathedral of St. John the Divine:

> When I returned to the church of my birth [Episcopalian] it was not to discard the intellect, but now I know that to depend on intellect alone is not enough. Perhaps it is because I am a storyteller that I need sign, symbol, sacrament, that which takes me beyond where my mind can go alone.[10]

There is probably no clearer demonstration of Madeleine's need for the liturgy and symbolism of the church than in *The Irrational Season*. Here she suggests that, because we cannot comprehend the nature of the universe and of God with our finite minds, it is only through the language of symbol, metaphor, myth, and story that we can approach these mysteries.

Structured around the Christian calendar, the twelve chapters of *The Irrational Season* describe Madeleine's understanding of each "irrational season" of the church's liturgical year. Pointing out that beginnings only come after endings, Madeleine begins and ends the book with the season of Advent, the start of the church's year. The Christmas season is particularly special to Madeleine. When Hugh and Madeleine celebrated their second Christmas together, their daughter, Josephine, was just six months old. Madeleine wrote in *The Irrational Season* that

> the beautiful flesh of our child made the whole miracle of incarnation new.[11]

This reference to incarnation reflects on what continues to be a key element of Madeleine's theology: the revelation of God in Jesus Christ. Each year at Christmastime, the Franklin/L'Engle Christmas letter contains a poem by Madeleine expressing the awe she feels about the birth of the Holy Child. *Christmas Love, 1992* is one example:

Thank you, God, for being born,
You who first invented birth
(Universe, galaxies, the earth).
When your world was tired & worn
You came laughing on the morn.
Thank you, most amazing Word
For your silence in the womb
Where there was so little room
Yet the still small voice was heard
Throughout a planet dark & blurred.
Merry Christmas! Wondrous day!
Maker of the universe.
You the end, & you the source
come to share in human clay
And, yourself, to show the Way.[12]

Just as special for Madeleine are the observations of Holy Week. In *The Irrational Season,* she describes the grim, dark, deeply moving Maundy Thursday service at the Cathedral, which serves as a reminder of Jesus' death.[13] Good Friday and Easter are intimately woven together in Madeleine's thinking, just as they are in the church year. For her, however, the emphasis is always on the resurrection, the affirmation of life that comes with Easter morning.[14]

Perhaps the church sacrament most meaningful to Madeleine is the celebration of Communion. In *The Rock That Is Higher,* she tells readers,

> When I receive Communion I am partaking in the most sacred myth and ritual of the Christian church (and let us remember that myth is about *truth*). When we receive the bread and the wine we receive the truth of Jesus' promise, the truth of his love. We don't need to get hung up on words like *transubstantiation,* which tend to take the Eucharist out of the truth of myth and into the wimpiness of fact. What happens when we receive the bread and wine is a mystery, and when we try to explain it in any kind of way we destroy our own ability to partake in the truth of this marvelous and eternally mysterious ritual.[15]

Part of what makes the Eucharist unique for Madeleine is that the communion table is a place where people can be known, accepted, and loved. She views this ritual as a place where we can find our common humanity, our woundedness can be accepted, and we can experience forgiveness. *The Irrational Season* contains a poem, written after a small dinner party, that expresses Madeleine's thoughts about this special gathering around the table:

> Sitting around your table
> as we did, able
> to laugh, argue, share
> bread and wine and companionship, care
> about what someone else was saying, even
> if we disagreed passionately: Heaven,
> we're told, is not unlike this, the banquet celestial,
> eternal convivium. So the *praegustum terrestrium*
> partakes—for me, at least—of sacrament. . . .
>
> Dare we come together, then, vulnerable, open, free?
> Yes! Around your table we
> knew the Holy Spirit, come to bless
> the food, the host, the hour, the willing guest.[16]

Along with *The Irrational Season, A Severed Wasp* is probably the best source of Madeleine's views about the church. The events of this novel are set almost entirely in the environs of the Cathedral of St. John the Divine. Mirroring Madeleine's involvement in the Cathedral—her participation in its activities, her teaching at her children's school St. Hilda's and St. Hugh's School, her volunteer work as the librarian—the characters in *A Severed Wasp* revolve around the church and church activities.

Though the protagonist of *A Severed Wasp,* Katherine Vigneras, is not a churchgoer, through her eyes the reader observes not only the ambiguity of human nature (both in the present and through her flashbacks) but also the limitations of the church through Katherine's friendship with Felix Bodeway, a retired bishop of the Cathedral.

It is not surprising to find ministers in Madeleine's fiction, given that ministers have long peopled the pages of her real life. In particular, during Madeleine's first years back in New York after returning from the Crosswicks period in Connecticut, she became acquainted with Canon Edward West at the Cathedral of St. John the Divine. This was a time of questioning for Madeleine. As she pondered the problem of suffering, the nature of God, and the meaning of existence, she turned to Canon West for guidance. Canon West not only became her spiritual advisor but a great friend to the entire Franklin family. Being present during many family crises and celebrations, he served for the rest of his life as minister *extraordinaire* to them.[17]

The ministers who populate Madeleine's books reflect her attitude toward ministry. In *A Severed Wasp*, we learn that Bishop Felix Bodeway hears confessions during his years at the Cathedral, he visits the poor and the sick, he evokes trust, and he keeps confidences well. However, we not only meet a minister who is dedicated and humble; we also find a human being who is scared, scarred, and imperfect.

In an early scene in *A Severed Wasp*, Felix is in the nave of the Cathedral. He has invited Katherine to dine with him in an effort to renew an old friendship and to ask her, as a retired concert pianist, to give a benefit performance at the Cathedral. Katherine notes that this stooped and frail old man is quite different from the "lightweight" person she knew in her late teens.

Both Felix and Katherine appeared as younger characters in Madeleine's *The Small Rain*. In the interim years, something has happened to change Felix. In *A Severed Wasp*, he makes a long confession of his unsavory past to Katherine, certain that she will hear, understand, and accept him. He tells of a failed marriage, some questionable relationships, and the horror of his wartime experiences, confessing that it was when he was at the pit of despair and disappointment that he felt the call of God to the priesthood. He explains that, when he learned to accept himself just as he was, as a person who *already* had God's love, he discovered his vocation to the priesthood.[18]

Through the vehicle of Felix's story, Madeleine reiterates her conviction that God calls ordinary people, not the pious and pure, to do God's work. In Felix, Madeleine allows us to see something of her ideas about the working of God's grace in human lives, reminding us that priests and ministers are first of all fallible human beings. Through Felix, Madeleine voices the human need for God's grace.

As the story continues, Katherine and her friend (and tenant) Mimi Oppenheimer are invited to the deanery for refreshments after attending an organ concert in the Cathedral. Here Bishop Undercroft reads the quotation from George Orwell's *Collected Essays* that gives *A Severed Wasp* its name. The passage tells of Orwell's having cut a wasp in half as it sat on his plate. The wasp went on eating jam, not realizing it was mortally wounded until it tried to fly away.

Undercroft's comments after reading the passage reflect Madeleine's view of the church:

> "It's all too easy to see the Church in that image, the greedy wasp unaware of its brokenness. And I don't mean just the Episcopal Church which still hasn't rid itself of its image—"

> "God's frozen people," Bishop Juxon murmured.

> Undercroft nodded, "It's also the Romans, the Evangelicals, the Pentecostals, all of us who believe we profess Christ."[19]

Felix enters the conversation at this point, adding,

> "Once we recognize that we're broken, we have a chance to mend."[20]

Because Madeleine recognizes that the church is broken, that the community of the church reflects the humanness (and therefore the imperfections) of its participants, it is no surprise when Felix reports blackmail, threatening phone calls, violence, drugs, jealousy, and revenge motives among the members of the Cathedral family. *A Severed Wasp* is indeed about a wounded, imperfect institution, and yet an institution to which Madeleine is totally devoted. Though not perfect, one can hear her say, the church is the best religious institution we have and sometimes it works wonders. Perfection is not what she expects or desires from the church, but rather understanding, compassion, forgiveness, and acceptance.

In *A Severed Wasp* Katherine, the "unchurched" protagonist, is presented in the roles of both confessor and mediator to Felix Bodeway, who is steeped in the Anglican tradition of confession and absolution. He thinks of Katherine as a confessor *extraordinaire* and in so doing, pays tribute to the power of forgiveness, even from an apparently agnostic layperson. Forgiveness—and the question of who is "qualified" to forgive—is one of the main themes of *A Severed Wasp*. Madeleine believes firmly that all who know their own need of forgiveness, and who have experienced forgiveness and love, can forgive others. She accepts as true the priesthood of *all* believers.

Madeleine introduces two new ministers to her readers in *A Live Coal in the Sea*: Mac Xanthakos, Camilla Dickinson's husband, and Art Xanthakos, Mac's father. In both cases, they are presented as people of deep faith but very human and flawed. Both have experienced suffering and are aware of their own shortcomings. The themes of repentance, forgiveness, and grace are central to this book in which Madeleine continues to underscore the importance of the church—with the recognition that neither the church nor its ministers is perfect, nor do its ministers have a corner on the market of "priesting."

On Sundays, when she is in New York City, Madeleine attends All Angels Episcopal Church and also participates in a house church related to the All Angels' congregation. When in Connecticut, she attends the Congregational Church. When I have visited Madeleine with other friends in her New York apartment, we have worshipped together using the Episcopal *Book of Common*

Prayer and celebrated Communion together. One of her favorite sources of worship is the *New Zealand Prayer Book.*

In *Friends for the Journey,* Madeleine and Luci Shaw share their experiences of prayer and worship and relate how important this aspect is to their long and close friendship. They call it "coming together before God."[21] They pray spontaneously together, even over the telephone. The Church, for Madeleine, is the gathered fellowship of believers, whether it is Madeleine with her house-mate, Barbara, or with Luci Shaw or another friend gathered two-by-two to say evening prayers together.

Ultimately, Madeleine L'Engle is an ecumenist: She believes in the universal church and is pained by the arrogance, narrowness, and lack of love in individuals and groups who would separate and divide this body. She wishes that each branch of Christendom would consider other denominations as "sister institutions" and accept the members of other religious communities at their communion sacraments. She sees the differing interpretations as finite, inadequate, and imperfect human efforts to understand that which is infinite. She believes that unity in affirming the "mystery of the Word made flesh" is much stronger than whatever else divides believers.[22]

When conducting conferences at Aqueduct Conference Center in Chapel Hill, North Carolina, Madeleine often requests the celebration of communion. The service is inclusive, ecumenical, and rich with depth and meaning for everyone: A Methodist minister or an Episcopalian priest may conduct the service, Madeleine helps to serve the host, and the partakers are Christians from many denominations.

I have a vivid memory of an occasion during a creative writing course Madeleine was teaching at Mundelein College in Chicago, when she said, "Let's have the Holy Eucharist." In this ecumenical gathering, I, a Presbyterian minister, was the officiant; a lay reader in the Catholic church assisted; and several of the nuns who taught and administered at this Roman Catholic institution worshipped with us.

Through her church participation, memberships, and speaking engagements, Madeleine embodies her ecumenical hope. She has addressed every mainline denominational group: Protestant and Catholic, evangelical and liberal. Although her "letter of membership" remains with the Congregational Church in Goshen, Connecticut, she considers herself a member of the informal All Angels Episcopal Church in New York, where she worships on Sunday, serves on the vestry, and participates in a house church. She also considers herself part of the community of the Cathedral of St. John the Divine, participating regularly in the daily noontime celebration of the Eucharist. She can and does worship anywhere, but in the Episcopal church, her love of symbol, liturgy, and sacrament finds a home. She asks rhetorically, "Why can't I belong to more than one church?"[23] and reminds us where the church is found:

> Not the building in which I stand or sit, often uncomfortably, often irritably. Not any denomination of any kind—and the fact that the Body of Christ is broken by denominations is another cause for Satan's pleasure. Why can't we worship in our differing ways and still be One?[24]

Madeleine continues to hope for the reunification of the church, not to homogenize churches or surrender the unique liturgical characteristics of her beloved Anglican church, but rather for recognition and acceptance of one another with humility and love. She laments the church's reluctance to change or admit when it does not have answers, and she acknowledges that the church is not very good at change.[25] But she also recognizes that change does slowly happen. The church once taught that the earth was flat and the center of the universe; it condemned Galileo as a heretic for proving Copernicus's theory that the earth revolved around the sun. It has even changed within this century its teaching about the nature of God:

It is now generally acknowledged that God, rather than being aloof and impervious, is more like the suffering servant of Isaiah.[26]

At the same time, she cautions against change that is so fast it destroys the institution:

> If we change our understanding through our attempts at definition, we will also radically change the church institution as it has continually evolved over the centuries. There comes a moment when all institutions need changing, but such change is inevitably fraught with danger. It can be disastrous as well as creative, and once we admit that change is needed, we are open to both possibilities.[27]

In *The Rock That Is Higher,* Madeleine reveals her wish that the church would more willingly admit that there are some questions of faith it cannot answer. She ingenuously observes

> there are no answers to the wonder of Creation, the marvel of the Incarnation, the glory of the Resurrection.[28]

For Madeleine, there are no answers to questions about the infinite; there are only declarations of faith. She believes it is the responsibility of the church to proclaim the wonders of the *mysterium tremendum et fascinans* and the confidence that El will be ultimately victorious.

Through the example of her faithfulness to the church as an institution, Madeleine encourages readers to see that the church is in process and not give up hope. Ultimately, she encourages us to face the imperfections of our churches and to work within their structures to make changes. When I asked her what she thought were the greatest accomplishments and strengths of the universal church, she replied,

> It has survived. It provides community for people. And, it is a place where it is likely one will hear both the immanence and transcendence of God proclaimed at the same time.[29]

In the closing scene of *A Severed Wasp*, Katherine Vigneras is giving a benefit performance in the sanctuary of the Cathedral of St. John the Divine. In the moments before the concert, problems resolved and sins forgiven, the citizens of the church environs are waiting for her to begin. The silence that precedes the performance conveys a sense of the communion that Madeleine treasures.

Four years after *A Severed Wasp* was published, Hugh Franklin became ill with cancer. Unlike Madeleine's experience during her father's illness and death, this time she was not alone with her pain and grief. Long an inextricable part of her daily life, the church community emerged in force to support her. In *Two-Part Invention: The Story of a Marriage*, Madeleine records some of these events.

The rector at the Trinity Episcopal Church in Torrington, Connecticut, visited Hugh daily in the hospital.[30] The minister at the Congregational Church in Goshen also visited and prayed. When Hugh died, his funeral service was held on a Sunday at the Goshen church, and a Eucharist was celebrated at Trinity Church on Monday. Hugh's life was further celebrated in New York in a requiem mass conducted by Canon West at the Cathedral. The wider community of hundreds of Madeleine's and Hugh's friends embraced her with their telephone calls, cards, and prayers.

Three years after Hugh's death, Canon West died. This was another inexpressible loss for Madeleine, and another testimony to the importance of the church in her life. Madeleine was invited to deliver the eulogy for Canon West at a requiem mass held in the Cathedral. Perhaps more than any other person, Canon West had brought the church into Madeleine's life through his sustaining friendship, guidance, and love over the years:

> If at death we are to be judged on this life, then what we do here and now matters enormously. It may be of ultimate import whether or not we give a thirsty child a cup of cold water, whether or not we feed the hungry stranger who comes to our door. St. John of the Cross said, "In the evening of life we shall be judged on love."[31]

For Madeleine L'Engle, the final measure of the church—and of our lives, whether in or out of the church—is whether we have shown love in our relationships with others:

> When we are once more known for our love, we will be the hope of the world, and we will bear the light.[32]

CHAPTER VII

The Butterfly Effect

We have much to be judged on . . .
slums and battlefields and insane asylums,
but these are the symptoms of our illness,
and the result of our failures in love.
In the evening of life we shall be judged on love,
and not one of us is going to come off very well.[1]

Dolphins and butterflies . . . lightning bugs and weeping willows . . . all parts of the whole of Creation. This is how Madeleine L'Engle sees the universe: Every living thing, made by a loving God, is intimately and miraculously interconnected with and dependent upon every other.

> We are indeed part of a universe. We belong to each other; the fall of every sparrow is noted, every tear we shed is collected in the Creator's bottle.[2]

From reading about the amazing discoveries of astrophysicists, particle physicists, and cellular biologists for more than thirty years, Madeleine has concluded that perhaps the most challenging scientific discovery of this century was the exposure of the heart of the atom. The dark side of that event was the knowledge that made destruction possible through nuclear fission. But the bright and hopeful side is the "vision of the interrelatedness" and oneness of all that is.[3] Madeleine believes that our fragmented planet desperately needs this vision of an interdependent Creation. She often speaks of this interrelatedness as "the butterfly effect":

> In a recent article on astrophysics I came across the beautiful and imaginative concept known as "the butterfly effect." If a butterfly winging over the fields around Crosswicks should be hurt, the effect would be felt in galaxies thousands of light years away. The interrelationship of all of Creation is sensitive in a way we are just beginning to understand. If a butterfly is hurt, we are hurt. If the bell tolls, it tolls for us.[4]

Troubling a Star, Madeleine's recent novel about Vicky Austin, provides Madeleine with another opportunity to underline her belief in the interconnectedness of all things. Even the title of the book reflects the butterfly effect. In this story, Vicky Austin has gone to Antarctica to visit her friend Adam Eddington, who is doing research at an outpost there. Vicky runs into trouble and that creates the plot of the novel. During her voyage south, her ship stops near the Falkland Islands and passengers go ashore in small boats called kodiaks. Once they are ashore, Siri, one of Vicky's new friends, takes out a small harp and begins to accompany herself to a song:

> All things by immortal power,
> Near or far,
> Hiddenly
> To each other linked are,
> That thou canst not stir a flower
> Without troubling a star.[5]

The social and moral consequences of such an interconnection are played out fully in *A Live Coal in the Sea*. A pregnant and troubled Camilla tries to relax to music and, hearing the sounds of the dryer spinning and the refrigerator being opened and closed, reflects,

> If the centrifugal force of the dryer is dependent on the fixed start, so is the life of that baby born of my dead mother and God knows what father . . . so is the life of my own infant swimming so gently inside me in the amniotic fluid. So is Mac. And Frank. And Mama and Papa. So am I. We cannot do anything in isolation. It is all interconnection.[6]

Threaded throughout Madeleine's writing is the belief that with the awareness of interconnectedness comes a responsibility: We need to respond to the problems that trouble the entire planet, and every one of our actions or reactions has an effect.

> Perhaps what we are called to do may not seem like much, but the butterfly is a small creature to affect galaxies thousands of light years away.[7]

For Madeleine, this translates into a heightened awareness of the potential effects of her writing. She believes that neither she nor any other writer can write "without including, whether we intend to or not, our response to the world around us"[8] and its response to us. Although not a political activist who celebrates her causes through writing, Madeleine L'Engle uses her stories to convey her views about injustice in its many forms, from environmental pollution to war and prejudice.

If the planet belongs to all earth dwellers, then Madeleine's concern for the environment is a logical consequence: She believes it is imperative that we not waste the resources of our earth. I saw this concern demonstrated firsthand when I visited Madeleine at Crosswicks. Long before recycling was a common household practice, Madeleine's kitchen contained bins for glass and aluminum and other recyclables. I watched her matter-of-factly open a can, cut the bottom out, stick the lids inside the can, and squash it flat before she placed it in the appropriate bin.

Madeleine's efforts at recycling stem from her persuasion that human greed

> is consuming the planet, so that we may quite easily kill this beautiful earth by daily pollution without ever having nuclear warfare.[9]

She views our "acceptance of ourselves as consumers"[10] as one of the root causes of pollution. In fact, she dislikes even the word "consumer," which means literally to "use up," as in forest fires consuming land and trees and wildlife, careless developers and farmers consuming rain forests, drugs and disease consuming people.[11] Rather than consuming the world, Madeleine believes, we have been placed by God on this planet to be stewards, observers, and creators.

A Wind in the Door, the second fantasy in *The Time Trilogy,* contains one of Madeleine L'Engle's clearest statements about the destruction humans are wreaking upon the earth. Charles Wallace's life depends on his sister Meg and two friends persuading a farandola named Sporos to root or "deepen." Meg tries to communicate with Senex, the mature farandola from whom Sporos has sprung, but gets no response. The cherubim Proginoskes assures her that Senex is aware that Charles Wallace is seriously ill. When she asks *how* Senex knows, Proginoskes answers,

> "As you know that your Earth is ill, by fish dying in the rivers, birds dying in the forests, people dying in the choked cities. You know by war and hate and chaos. Senex knows [Charles Wallace's] mitochondrion is ill because the farandolae will not Deepen and many farae are dying."[12]

Madeleine also expresses her concern about human disregard for the environment in *A Ring of Endless Light,* sharing insights about simple things we might do to take care of the earth. At the outset, readers learn of the Austins' care for the *whole* family of God, including even the smallest creatures. No one in the family, for example, uses the front door of Grandfather's Seven Bay Island home for fear of disturbing a nest of baby swallows just above it.[13]

The Austins' concern for earth's creatures appears throughout the book. A poignant scene occurs when Suzy reads a newspaper article about thousands of dolphins being clubbed to death. She is upset almost to the point of tears. When family members point out that this was done by people who depend on fish for their livelihood because the porpoises were eating the fish, Suzy counters with,

> "Porpoises don't hurt anybody. They don't murder or have wars. They don't pollute the environment."[14]

Through Suzy's concern for the dolphins, Madeleine expresses her belief that all creatures belong in this world and need to be protected.

One of Vicky Austin's friends during this Seven Bay Island summer is Adam Eddington, who is working with dolphins in a marine biology lab. At one point a dolphin named Enid loses her newborn baby. This event upsets everyone who knows Enid, especially Vicky. In an expression of her grief, Vicky composes a sonnet that reflects in general the sadness experienced by Suzy and the entire Austin family about the slaughter of dolphins and in particular her own grief at the loss of Enid's baby:

> The earth will never be the same again.
> Rock, water, tree, iron, share this grief
> As distant stars participate in pain.
> A candle snuffed, a falling star or leaf,
> A dolphin death, O this particular loss
> Is Heaven-mourned; for if no angel cried,
> If this small one was tossed away as dross,
> The very galaxies then would have lied.

How shall we sing our love's song now
In this strange land where all are born to die?
Each tree and leaf and star show how
The universe is part of this one cry,
That every life is noted and is cherished,
And nothing loved is ever lost or perished.[15]

This sonnet illustrates not only Madeleine's convictions about the importance of the particular but also her response to the beauty of the earth. Living in a universe created by a loving God means, for Madeleine, that we have the responsibility to love and "hallow" nature:

> Hallowing means being made whole and holy by the grace of the Holy Spirit, not by our own effort. It is heaven's gift. So our observing and contemplating needs to be hallowed, or we will fail in that for which we have been called.[16]

At the opposite end of the spectrum from hallowing is desecrating. Madeleine L'Engle's disdain for desecration of nature by what she calls "technocracy"[17] is evident in a dialogue between Vicky and her friend Zachary. Through Zachary's description of the cryonics process by which his deceased mother's body has been frozen, Madeleine voices her protest against the artificiality and phoniness of the consumerism that adds to the ugliness and pollution of the environment. Through Vicky's response to Zachary, Madeleine conveys her dismay about the abuse of technology used to deep-freeze the dead and create plastic grass:[18]

> Into my mind's eye flashed an image of the afternoon before, when we were standing by a dark hole in the ground, waiting for Commander Rodney's body to be lowered into it. Somehow that struck me as being more realistic than being deep-frozen. Being deep-frozen went along with plastic grass and plastic earth and trying to pretend that death hadn't really happened.[19]

Later in the story, Vicky and Leo, Commander Rodney's oldest son, go to the hospital to give blood for Vicky's grandfather. It is raining, and Vicky lifts her face to catch raindrops with her tongue. Leo warns her that rainwater is no longer pure enough to drink:

> "It's got lots of nasties in it now from the gluck we've put in the atmosphere, strontium 90 and other radioactive horrors."[20]

Vicky responds violently, "I hate it!"[21] The youngsters explore the possible connection between a growing number of cases of leukemia and increased pollution, a concern Madeleine shares.[22]

Madeleine's conviction that pollution and disease are linked is also reflected in *Certain Women*. Two women, Abby and Alice, are discussing David Wheaton's cancer. Abby is struggling to understand why David, who never smoked and rarely drank, should get cancer. Alice observes that it might be because human beings are living longer, but she also points out,

> "If we're not killed in some kind of accident, it's likely cancer will get us in the end, particularly as we go on polluting our planet."[23]

It is not only *human* illnesses that concern Madeleine. She reminds readers in this same book that the land is sick because of the damage humans are doing to the forests. Sitting on the boat *Portia* with her dying father, Emma Wheaton looks back at the shore and the scars on the hillside:

> She looked with loathing at the brown scars, acres of land where the trees had been indiscriminately logged, with only a small fringe of evergreen left at the waterline to disguise the carnage.[24]

Perhaps one of Madeleine's most probing questions about our unthinking destruction of the land—and, ultimately, of ourselves —appears in *Sold into Egypt*:

How could human creatures who have truly observed the beauty of the planet, who have enjoyed the world aright then proceed to foul it with greed and stupidity and pollution? With the ugliness of inner cities which surely bear no resemblance to the Celestial City? With strip mining and deforestation and smoke belching from factory chimneys—and how much of the increase in cancer comes from polluted food and air and water?[25]

Bright Evening Star also includes a statement by Madeleine about the importance of taking care of nature. She views the incarnation of God in the form of Christ as an affirmation of God's care for the earth, and she bemoans the attitude of those who are so focused on "the afterlife" that they do not see the need to protect and conserve the environment we have now.[26] When Jesus poses the question, "Do you want to be made whole?" Madeleine believes our answer should include the wholeness of our entire society and environment.[27]

Human destruction comes in many forms, and it does not stop with killing dolphins or the land: We humans seem bent on destroying each other in the form of war. It comes as no surprise that Madeleine L'Engle has much to say about war, since the first war victim she knew was a member of her immediate family. During World War I, which was thought incorrectly to have been the "war to end all wars," Madeleine's father was poisoned with mustard gas that destroyed his lungs and eventually took his life when she was seventeen. Her hatred of war and what war does to people and civilizations is rooted in this early experience.

Madeleine reinforces her point that war is hell by affirming the extraordinary value of human life. In *Camilla,* one of Madeleine's earliest novels, the teenage protagonist, Camilla, is suffering through a family crisis. Her friend Frank takes her to see his friend David, who has been injured in a war. David has lost his legs and has not been able to wear artificial legs because of severe stomach wounds. As David and Frank discuss death and destruction, Camilla observes that both of them are so full of life that she feels hopeful.[28] David affirms this by saying that, though there will always be war,

> "life is the greatest gift that could ever be conceived. . . . A daffodil pushing up through the dark earth to the spring, knowing somehow deep in its roots that spring and light and sunshine will come, has more courage and more knowledge of the value of life than any human being I've met."[29]

David concludes by urging Camilla to model herself after the daffodil.

Madeleine explores war more extensively in *A Severed Wasp*. Although this story has a contemporary setting, the horror of the Nazi concentration camps casts its long shadow over the narrative through the memory of the protagonist, concert pianist Katherine Vigneras. Within days of her marriage to Justin Vigneras, also a pianist, Katherine was taken to a makeshift camp and Justin to Auschwitz. Katherine was beaten on the back but her hands were spared. Justin's captors crushed his hands so badly that he never played again. He also suffered an injury that made it impossible for him to father children. This changed the entire course of their lives and their marriage.

Through flashbacks, as Katherine remembers and relives her days of terror during the war, we are reminded of the stupidity and horror of humanity's inhumanity to itself. In one flashback scene, Katherine and Justin come to Berlin after the war to give a concert. Their hotel room overlooks a square that has been partly demolished by bombs. As Katherine looks out a window, she sees a landscape "filled with rubble, with barbed wire, with gaping holes." She sees children playing ball in the square and laughing. But they are not ordinary children: They are missing limbs.[30] The view horrifies Katherine, and she turns to Justin, telling him she had not realized what the bombing by the Americans had done:

"Oh, God, Justin, I wanted to kill, personally with my bare hands, the people at Auschwitz. I'd have done it gladly—but not this—this random maiming of children and old people and—"[31]

When Justin responds coldly that the American attack was only justice, Katherine continues:

"There's a little boy out in the square; he's bouncing a ball with his foot because he doesn't have any arms. He didn't have anything to do with Auschwitz."[32]

Justin is neither sympathetic nor understanding of Katherine's horror. He responds in an emotionless voice:

"Don't be naïve. You should have learned something about war by now. The innocent always suffer. What did you want your country to do? Sit back and let the Nazis take over the world so that we'd all be in a series of concentration camps from Alaska to Africa? That's the alternative. Is that what you want?"[33]

Through this dialogue, Madeleine makes clear not only her horror of war but also her awareness of the ambiguity and complexity of our choices with regard to war. She reluctantly accepts that war is sometimes an unavoidable choice between two wrongs, the lesser of two evils, but she firmly believes that it is *never* right. Even under the best of circumstances, innocent people are killed and maimed. Above all, even when war seems an inescapable choice, she insists, it must never be glorified, and we must do what we do prayerfully and repent of the evil we do.[34] I have heard Madeleine say more than once that the soul of the United States cannot get well until we apologize to Japan and to the world for dropping atomic bombs on its cities. And she certainly understands that Vietnam did not leave our hands clean.[35]

In *The Rock That Is Higher*, Madeleine repeats the answer she gave a twelve-year-old who asked her in a letter, "Is it ever right to kill?":

Is it? What does this do to the family of God's human creatures? I graduated from college into the Second World War,
and that was not an ambiguous war; Hitler *had* to be stopped.
But what about all those bombs dropped on Germany? On
hospitals? On women and children who had nothing to do
with the war? Was all that necessary for the winning of the
war? That's one of many questions for which I have no answer. Sometimes we are in situations where there is no right
choice, and we have to make the choice which we prayerfully
believe to be the least wrong, never forgetting that it is
wrong.[36]

What can we do to prevent war? Madeleine writes stories and
suggests that we pray, believing that both stories and prayer send
out positive energy that God can use to accomplish El's purpose.[37]
She believes that

> the power of prayer is greater than the Pentagon . . . greater
> than the bomb. It can help bring wisdom to our knowledge,
> wisdom which is all that will keep us from destroying ourselves
> with our knowledge.[38]

At the root of Madeleine's attitude about war lies the same
conviction she has expressed about pollution and consumption of
the environment: that every human being is part of one interconnected family. At the most basic level, she believes that family
members simply should not hurt other family members. She sees
human self-centeredness, or our lack of caring for each other, as
leading to the destructive choices that bring suffering. She makes
this point in *Sold into Egypt*:

> It seems odd that those who take the anthropic view seem not
> to have noticed that we have made a mess of it, with our lack
> of joy, our overblown sense of self-importance. How could hu-
> man creatures who have truly observed and contemplated a
> child, any child, then blast that child with napalm? How
> could anyone who has ever loved anybody plant a bomb in a
> plane and wantonly kill several hundred people?[39]

Madeleine's message is that war is hell, not only because bombs and bullets wreak catastrophic damage upon cities and people, but also because of what war does to our *spirit*. No member of the human family escapes the horror of war.

But Madeleine points out a more subtle, if not equal, destruction of the human spirit: prejudice, especially racial prejudice. If all creatures in the universe are interdependent, it is logical, she believes, to conclude that people of all races belong in this universe, that all human beings are brothers and sisters.

In *The Summer of the Great-grandmother*, the story of Madeleine's mother's last summer, Madeleine tells of the relationship between her mother's great-grandmother, called Greatie, and an African princess whom a wealthy slave trader and planter had married and brought to live in north Florida. Greatie made friends with the princess and once a week was rowed down the river, a two- to three-hour trip, to visit her. Madeleine celebrates their unique friendship:

> Greatie and the princess were close friends in a day when such a friendship was unheard of, and Greatie simply laughed when she was criticized and sometimes slandered because of this relationship. I was delighted when I learned only recently, that a good friend of mine is a descendant of this long-gone African princess.[40]

Madeleine also fictionalized Greatie's friendship with the princess in her novel *The Other Side of the Sun*. In this story set in the South, the elderly Stella Reiner has returned to the family home, Illyria, with the task of deciding its fate. As Stella reflects on her first days at Illyria, she reminisces about an African princess named Honoria, who was the original owner of Illyria and with whom Stella's husband's grandmother, Mado, was great friends.[41]

As Stella reads Mado's journal, she learns more about the friendship between Mado and Honoria and their belief that they were different but equal. The horror and stupidity of racism in the

Old South are clearly spelled out in Honoria's story. She is a strong, self-assured, humble, but proud woman who, though she owns Illyria, acts as a servant in the house because property ownership by black persons could not be acknowledged in the South in those days.

Ultimately, Madeleine's view of injustice, whether environmental pollution, war, or prejudice, is one of measured consideration and thoughtfulness. Her prescription is to increase our awareness of what is unjust, respond with love and understanding, and stay open to new revelations about the nature of God and the way things are supposed to be.[42]

Madeleine's more recent writings seem to be addressing some of the harsh and hard realities of human existence, such as sexual promiscuity and homosexuality. Such overt attention, of necessity, involves a clarification of her unhappiness with the religious fundamentalism whose teachings include a judgmental, harsh God. In the decade of the nineties, I believe Madeleine has taken off her velvet gloves.

Homosexuality was a very minor theme in *A Severed Wasp*. There was some reference to the homosexual experiences of Bishop Felix Bodeway and of the husband of Dorcas, Katherine Vigneras' boarder. The pain caused by and to these characters by their sexual orientation was portrayed without judgment or apparent resolution. However, in *A Live Coal in the Sea*, readers meet a school teacher, who is a homosexual, and he is portrayed as a moral, spiritual, wise, and very kind individual whose advice helps to redeem the marriage relation of Olivia Xanthakos. In fact, it is into the mouth of this young teacher that Madeleine puts the words about the grace of God from which the title of this novel is taken.[43]

For decades Madeleine has written passionately about the God of love, but it is in *A Live Coal in the Sea* that she directly confronts the condemnatory voices of religious fundamentalists. With her reputation as a devout Christian and deeply spiritual woman, Madeleine has little to lose in her efforts to remind her readers that the

Christian family is about love and grace, not hate and judgment.

Madeleine sometimes uses the analogy of the fairy tale, most recently in *The Rock That Is Higher,* to make her point. Using the familiar story of the princess and the pea, she identifies the "true princess" as one who is so sensitive to the pains and injustices of the world (the pea under a large stack of mattresses) that she is kept awake all night. By staying awake to injustice, Madeleine believes, the "true princess" in each of us can make a difference in the world:

> Simply the fact that we couldn't sleep all night because we felt the hard pea of awareness under all these mattresses of indifference is a step in helping Christ overcome the world.[44]

Madeleine also suggests that the "true princess" (who in this story happens to be a storyteller) works to make other people aware of social ills. Although awareness itself is no guarantee of change, Madeleine is convinced that "if enough people become aware, then things can change for the better."[45] Awareness increases the chance that people will care, and out of caring comes love, and out of love comes social action.[46] The theme of love as the source for social action runs through all of Madeleine's stories, beginning with *A Wrinkle in Time* when Meg's love for Charles Wallace releases him from the monster, IT. Madeleine suggests that, if there is a monster within us that causes and tolerates the evils we do in our world, then only love can release that monster.

There are many ways to "release the monster": Change can take many forms. But no matter the method, change is difficult. Madeleine understands that her straightforward writing about moral problems and social issues may upset some readers, but long ago she learned to be comfortable with her identity as a "universe-disturber":

> If we disturb the universe, no matter how lovingly, we're likely to get hurt. Nobody ever promised that universe-disturbers would have an easy time of it. Universe-disturbers make waves, rock boats, upset establishments.[47]

While Madeleine has her critics, she believes that she is making the best choice—and she is in good company:

> Jesus was a great universe-disturber, so upsetting to the establishment of his day that they put him on a cross, hoping to finish him off. Those of us who try to follow his Way have a choice, either to go with him as universe-disturbers (butterflies) or to play it safe. Playing it safe ultimately leads to personal diminishment and death. If we play it safe, we resist change. Well. We all resist change, beginning as small children with our unvarying bedtime routine, continuing all through our lives.[48]

When John Andriote, a writer for the *National Catholic Register,* interviewed Madeleine for an article in the column "Dialogue," he asked what she saw as the social obligation of an artist whose vision of society conflicts with the status quo. Madeleine reflected that in the sixties she had asked herself a similar question about her response to the civil rights movement: What *was* her responsibility? Should she hop on one of the buses leaving the Cathedral and head to a protest in Washington?

> "I got the answer loud and clear: 'No, Madeleine, stay at your typewriter; you'll reach more people that way.' Many of us speak more directly to the issues of injustice through our work than we ever would through political activism."[49]

For over fifty years, Madeleine L'Engle has stayed at her typewriter and, recently, her computer. She has told stories that firmly but gently seek to raise the consciousness of her readers about the disturbing conditions she finds in the world and the wonder and grace of a God she calls *mysterium tremendum.* Trusting in the innate goodness of the human heart, Madeleine believes that when we know what the problems are—and understand that every problem affects each of us as part of an interdependent whole—then we will work to bring justice and healing to individuals and to the earth.

CHAPTER VIII
Beyond Gender Myths

*Women must be very gentle with men
as they, as well as women, seek to regain
the lost wholeness for which they were destined.*[1]

The naturalness and grace with which Madeleine L'Engle weaves her stories, whether autobiographical or fictional, may have disguised the feminist affirmations that are laced throughout her writing. She expresses her opposition to sexism with the same conviction and concern that she voices her firm beliefs about the evils of racism, war, and environmental destruction. Through her characters, themes, and plots, Madeleine makes clear assertions about gender equality and points her readers toward a world where both men and women are strong and gentle, and are of equal value. Because stories can be received at the affective and intuitive level of the heart, Madeleine's statements about gender equality are subtle but nonetheless powerful.

When I first became interested in Madeleine's work, I wrote to her about my desire to write about her ideas from a feminist perspective. Her reply, in part, read,

> I was very lucky in being brought up as an only child in a completely nonsexist family, where it never occurred to me that there was any reason that I could not do anything I wanted to do.[2]

The all-girls' schools in which Madeleine spent her high school and college years opened doors for leadership opportunities that were not available to girls and women in co-educational institutions during the thirties and forties.

By the time Madeleine married, one of her books had been published and another accepted for publication. She jokingly remarks that, because she had two books published, she did not have to look up from the diapers and say to her husband, "Dear, I think I would like to be a writer." In an unusual arrangement for the forties, Hugh encouraged Madeleine to quit her acting work and write full-time, while they shared the housework and child care.

Because of who she is and the circles in which she moved, Madeleine was not directly affected by the prejudice of sexism until after Hugh died. She tells about her firsthand encounter with discrimination against women in *Sold into Egypt*:

> Our joint bank account was frozen, and I was made very aware that this is still a male-dominated and male-chauvinist society, less paternalistic, perhaps, than in Jacob's day, but equally male-oriented. Hugh and I had had that account for over twenty-five years, and yet I had to prove that I, Madeleine, the *ux*, the wife, in this case, was capable of having a bank account.[3]

When I asked Madeleine if she considered herself a feminist, she said, "Yes, in the true sense of the word." If a feminist is a person who believes in and advocates equal rights for both sexes in the economic, political, social, and religious senses, this certainly describes Madeleine. She is, however, not comfortable or in agreement with extreme positions that put down men or propose a matriarchy that would be as exclusive of men as patriarchy has been exclusive of women. In "Shake the Universe," an article about feminist spirituality that appeared in *Ms.* magazine, Madeleine wrote:

> My role as a feminist is not to compete with men in their world—that's too easy, and ultimately unproductive. My job is to live fully as a woman, enjoying the whole of myself and my place in the universe.[4]

By taking a closer look at her fiction, we get a clearer picture of what Madeleine L'Engle means by "living fully as a woman." Of more than a score of novels, all but three have female protagonists.[5] Most of the female characters in her stories are strong and assertive: The girls are skilled and play important roles in the stories; most of the women have educations, careers, husbands, and children.

In 1962, when *A Wrinkle in Time* was published, it was uncommon for a novel to have a female child protagonist. Madeleine said that it never occurred to her *not* to have one. The central character of *Wrinkle*, Meg Murry, who is in her early teens, excels in math and science. With this bit of information, Madeleine not only suggested that females could be good in math and science, but she also tacitly denied the prevailing myth that they could not. Meg's adventures bear witness to the possibility of girls having exciting experiences and playing important roles in cosmic events. Furthermore, Meg's mother has two Ph.D.s in science and has won a Nobel Prize.

In her latest fantasy, *An Acceptable Time,* Madeleine's protagonist, Polly O'Keefe, travels back in time to team up with another young woman, Anaral of the People of the Wind, to be a healer and peacemaker. Both characters are portrayed as courageous, strong, and intuitive.

Madeleine's stories often include more subtle reminders of

the accomplishments and abilities of women, as in her fantasy *Many Waters*. The protagonists, Dennys and Sandy Murry, Meg's twin brothers, are discussing the nature of humanity and the idea that, in spite of the "bad" ones, there have been some very special and great humans. They recite a list of scientists: Euclid, Pasteur, and Tycho Brahe. Then, Dennys says,

> "I think Meg would like us to mention Maria Mitchell. Wasn't she the first famous woman astronomer?"[6]

This is both pedagogy and consciousness-raising at their best. This passage sent me—and perhaps many other readers—to the library to look up Maria Mitchell.

The accomplishments of the women in Madeleine's stories are consistent with her belief that living fully is important for everyone. Yet she is well aware of the dilemmas faced by women dealing with marriage, family, and career. She speaks from personal experience in her nonfiction and autobiographical books of the choices these roles involve. She shares freely with her readers the joys she has known in marriage and motherhood as well as some of the stresses and strains. In *A Circle of Quiet*, she tells of her frustration and weariness as she sought to fulfill all of these roles. However, Madeleine has said again and again that she made her choices freely and has no regrets.

Mirroring her own career, the preponderance of professional women in Madeleine's fiction comes naturally. She addresses this phenomenon, in part, in *The Irrational Season:*

> The reason the mothers in my children's books are usually professional women, respected in their chosen fields, is that this is the kind of woman I've always known best. In my marriage, sexism has never been a barrier. So I realize that it's easy for me to be casual about the words for gender. If I had grown up in an atmosphere where the female was put down, where my sex was relegated to an inferior place, I would not be able to be so casual.[7]

Madeleine does not see the question of "family or career" as an either/or choice for women. She believes it is vitally important for women to have multiple options in their lives, along with the freedom and right to choose among them. She states this explicitly in *Walking on Water* when describing criticism she received about her story *A Swiftly Tilting Planet.* In this fantasy the bright, young protagonist from *Wrinkle,* Meg Murry, has become an adult and chosen homemaking as her career by

> marrying Calvin, having children, and quietly helping her husband with his work behind the scenes.[8]

Madeleine concludes:

> If women are to be free to choose to pursue a career as well as marriage, they must also be free to choose the making of a home and the nurture of a family as their vocation; that was Meg's choice, and a free one, and it was as creative a choice as if she had gone on to get a Ph.D. in quantum mechanics.[9]

In the books Madeleine wrote in the eighties and nineties, her female characters seem to exercise more options than they did in earlier books. In *A Severed Wasp,* Katherine Vigneras befriends her downstairs tenant, Dorcas, who is pregnant and comes to Katherine for help after discovering her husband is unfaithful. Dorcas has been thinking about how she would raise her child alone. She concludes that she will have to give up both her dreams: the dream of being a great dancer and the dream of having a beautiful marriage. Katherine tells Dorcas that she is very brave, and this conversation follows:

> [Dorcas:] "Not brave. Just realistic. About time I dropped my dreams of being a great dancer and having a beautiful marriage."

> [Katherine:] "Don't be too hard on yourself. It's good to set your sights high."

[Dorcas:] "The thing is, in New York, people all have to do or be something. Something with a name, like doctor or dancer or director. Mother and wife don't count."

[Katherine:] "If feminism means anything, it means that you're free to be a mother or a dancer, or both, whichever you choose."[10]

Madeleine's beliefs about freedom of choice in the matter of career and/or marriage are further modeled in several other characters in *A Severed Wasp*: Suzy Davidson, a physician with four children; Mimi Oppenheimer, an orthopedic surgeon who is single and middle-aged; and Katherine, who is not only a retired concert pianist but also a widow, parent, and grandparent.

Although most of Madeleine L'Engle's protagonists are female, all of her main characters, whether children or adults, women or men, are strong, self-actualizing people. She does not seek to right the gender imbalance of the centuries by belittling or downgrading males. Just as strong, accomplished women populate her books, so do strong, gentle men. One of the best examples of this is Grandfather Eaton in the Austin series. Grandfather has painted his favorite poetry on the walls of his home, and shares with his granddaughter Vicky his love of poetry and of beauty. He is not afraid of his own tears or those of others. He shows courage, even in facing his terminal illness.

Another of Madeleine's "gentle men" is Bishop Felix Bodeway, Katherine Vigneras's friend in *A Severed Wasp*. Felix is presented not only as a strong individual who has faced hardships and challenges and has persevered, but also as a man in touch with his feminine side. He is able to express his fears, doubts, and feelings to Katherine, to share himself with her.

Bishop Colubra, of *An Acceptable Time*, is also in touch with his feminine side, particularly his intuition, which leads him to visit the distant past through the Time Door. Vicky's father qualifies as another of Madeleine's sensitive men. In *Meet the Austins*, Dr.

Austin's firm, but gentle way of helping his children accept Maggy into their family demonstrates his empathy.

There are no "macho" male characters in Madeleine's stories, except perhaps Zachary Gray. However, he is not a true candidate because Madeleine considers him a work-in-progress who will ultimately be redeemed. She is critical of the strictly "masculine" point of view that exalts reason and devalues the "intuitive, the nurturing, the numinous—the spiritual, if you will" aspects of being.[11] Madeleine takes the view that we have inherited from humans who operated exclusively out of their "male," rational side a world damaged by war, stupidity, and greed.[12] She also faults the socialization of both men and women, and the circumstances of their lives, for the roles each plays in the patriarchal system:

> Women have been allowed to affirm the nurturing and the intuitive in themselves, whereas more often than not men have been forced by society to limit themselves to the rational, fact-finding-and-proving part of their personalities. . . .

> As a woman, I deny my own free will if I blame men for the patriarchal society into which I was born. Males cannot take over unless females permit it. And in permitting it, we erode male wholeness as well as our own.[13]

Her compassion and concern for men are clearly evident in *And It Was Good*:

> Women must be very gentle with men as they, as well as women, seek to regain the lost wholeness for which they were destined.[14]

Madeleine sees one aspect of the "battle between the sexes" as an internal battle between our intuitive and intellectual parts.[15] Her writing bears witness to her conviction that women need to understand and claim the masculine within themselves, and men need to understand and accept the feminine within themselves. Herein lies one of her great appeals: She lifts people up, rather than putting them down. She ensures that her characters possess a balance of the best masculine and feminine qualities:

> Male and female, [we are] supposed to contain within ourselves the qualities of each.[16]

The people Madeleine considers "luminous" are those who use both their intellect and their intuition to the fullest.[17]

Madeleine illustrates this liberation in men, as well as women. In *A Stone for a Pillow*, she describes the incident where Jacob first meets Rachel at the well and weeps. This suggests that men once wept freely, before "civilization" taught them that tears are unmanly. Jacob, she writes,

> was sure enough of his own manhood that he was free to do all kinds of things which would be frowned on today. It's a freedom we all need to regain, and surely men are as much in need of liberation as women. Their chains are perhaps less visible, but easily as crippling.[18]

Noting the patriarchal nature of the Bible, she views the scriptural presentation of God as incomplete, partly because it is seen only through male eyes. She expresses this in *The Rock That Is Higher*:

> Scripture was written in a masculine world, which is a sign of things skewed and out of order. Where were the *daughters* of God? But we can't rewrite Scripture, though there have been some forlorn attempts to do so. The God of Scripture is seen through male eyes (Jacob, Moses, David), so what we are given is only a partial vision of God.[19]

However, given her conviction that God uses ordinary human beings, men *and* women, to accomplish El's work, it is not surprising that she has searched the Bible for stories of women's accomplishments:

Women did extraordinary things in Scripture. Deborah was one of the first judges. Esther was not only married to a king, she virtually ruled the country, and with an iron hand. Jael was a heroine, if a bloody one, in rescuing the Israelites from defeat in battle by driving a tent peg through the head of Sisera, their enemy. Certainly their stories helped me to hold high the image of women.[20]

Through the stories of these women, Madeleine confirms her dissatisfaction with the exclusiveness of biblical patriarchy, particularly as it is found in the Old Testament.

Without changing the text or violating the essence of the Bible, Madeleine L'Engle gives women a voice through *midrash*, a tradition of elaborating text with voices and thoughts from different people and historical contexts. These expanded commentaries allow her to present a feminist perspective of Scripture. For example, even in *Sold into Egypt*, which presents the patriarchal story about Joseph and his eleven brothers, five of the book's chapters end with a midrash in the voice of women: Leah's maid, Bildah; Leah's daughter, Dinah; Potiphar's wife; Gad's wife; and Joseph's wife, Asenath.

Dinah's midrash begins with a favorite benediction of the patriarchs: "Blessed art thou, O Lord our God, King of the universe, who has not made me a woman." It is followed by Dinah's angry response to the murder of Shechem, whom she loved:

Did anybody ask me whether I wanted to marry Shechem (Oh, my beautiful Shechem)? No. Nobody asked me. They cut him down and I flung myself on his bleeding body, and I don't think they even noticed me, they were so busy slaughtering everybody else.[21]

The midrash concludes with Dinah castigating the "war god" of the patriarchs, as she thinks of Shechem's gods:

If I knew who they were I would turn to them, and perhaps find more gentleness. Were they—are they—gods of war, gods of anger? . . . I would rather have a helpless god than a bloody one.[22]

In *The Rock That Is Higher*, Madeleine describes her early sense of the inclusive nature of God:

> When I was a child God was God. Because the eight-or-nine-year-old child does not think in terms of sex in general, neither did I in particular, and certainly not about God. God was All in all. God filled every single human need, be it for father, mother, lover, sister, brother, friend. Even when I became a "grown-up" I never thought of the God I prayed to as exclusively male.[23]

And It Was Good, her book about the beginning of the created universe and humanity, uses the scriptural text, "So God said, 'Let us make man in our image . . . male and female,' " to support her conclusion that "it takes both male and female to complete the image of God."[24] In the same book, Madeleine makes explicit her belief that God is *above* gender:

> One of the early words by which the ancient Hebrews knew God was El. El—the Lord. Beth-el, for instance, means the house of God. So I find it helpful, wherever and whenever possible, to call God El, or el, rather than using the masculine or feminine pronoun, because the name *El* lifts the Creator beyond all our sexisms and chauvinisms and anthropomorphisms.[25]

Perhaps Madeleine's fictional characters provide the most visible expression of her belief in the equality of women and men. She does this as a matter of course, as if she could not imagine people being any other way. In *A Ring of Endless Light*, for example, during a family dinner table discussion about a writer's use of the term "man," Suzy Austin asks, "What about women?" Mrs. Austin replies,

"Correct me if I'm wrong . . . but doesn't the Bible say, *So God created man in his own image, in the image of God created he him; male and female?* . . . So we females are half of mankind, Suzy, and don't let inverse sexism cheat you of your fair share."[26]

Although Madeleine was still using the term "mankind" when *A Ring of Endless Light* was published in 1980, it should be noted that she began to use inclusive language for humans and for God shortly after. However, her love of language and dislike of the artificial manipulation of language are obvious:

I, Madeleine, sex: f, wife and mother, am just as much *man* as is Hugh, sex: m, husband and father, and . . . I'm not about to abdicate my full share in mankind. One of the most pusillanimous things we of the female sex have done throughout the centuries is to have allowed the male sex to assume that *mankind* is masculine.

It is not. It takes both male and female to make the image of God. The proper understanding of mankind is that it is only a poor, broken thing if either male or female is excluded. The result of exclusion is that in terms of human sexuality the English language is presently inadequate. The word *man* has been so taken over by the male sex that I'm not sure it's redeemable.[27]

But often Madeleine finds no adequate substitutes for traditional, exclusive vocabulary. After considering some Old English terms, she concludes that she must tolerate the "present mutilated generic vocabulary." However, that does not stop her from creating nonsexist images of God. In *An Acceptable Time*, for instance, Anaral suggests some names for divinity:

"Starmaker, wind-breather, earth-grower, sun-riser, rain-giver."[28]

Madeleine does not advocate a contrived rewriting of the Bible to make it inclusive; however, she believes that both language and religion are like rivers, "constantly flowing from the same source, as we respond to all that is happening in the world around us."[29] Consequently, she believes evolutions and changes will come naturally and as needed in our language. Although Madeleine considers herself a feminist, her dislike of labels and pigeonholes would probably prevent her from calling herself an activist for women's rights. But through her stories, workshops, and teaching, she has had, and continues to have, an impact on the views women, men, and children take regarding gender.

Think of the matter-of-fact statement in *A Wrinkle in Time* that Mrs. Murry has two Ph.D.s and the later revelation in *A Swiftly Tilting Planet* that she has won a Nobel Prize. In the nineties, these achievements may seem rare but not impossible. However, *Wrinkle* was published a few years before Betty Friedan's *The Feminine Mystique,* and it has been sending these messages to children and adults for more than thirty years. We can only imagine the scope of the influence of Madeleine's quiet witness for gender equality in this book alone. And the story's popularity—with its much-needed messages for boys as well as girls—continues. Madeleine's reading of *The Time Trilogy* is available on audiocassettes, and Miramax Studios now has the production rights to make *A Wrinkle in Time* into a movie. Think of the influence these tapes and the film will have on new generations of children.

Madeleine's most recent fiction and nonfiction books continue to provide her with an opportunity to underscore her belief in gender equality. Her feminism remains firm and balanced. To Madeleine's list of female characters with Ph.D.s or M.D.s, such as Mrs. Murry and Mimi Oppenheimer, Madeleine adds Camilla Dickinson. In *A Live Coal in the Sea*, Camilla is a wife and mother, as well as an astronomer with a Ph.D., who has a career as a college professor. Even Camilla's mother-in-law, Olivia Xanthakos, is a strong character who has chosen to make being a wife and mother her life's work.

In a direct statement in *Bright Evening Star*, Madeleine writes,

> I am for inclusiveness, for understanding that God pronounced Adam and Eve to be male and female, made in the image of God, each different, each wonderful, each essential to the full image of the Maker.[30]

She refers to a book she had recently read that "suggested that Mary Magdalene was one of the apostles." While recognizing that the idea may shock some, Madeleine asks, "Why not?"[31]

> Why is this speculation about Mary Magdalene such a horrifying idea? From what we've been able to learn, it seems quite likely that she could have been one of the apostles, and she was surely one of the leading figures in the early church. It's not unimportant that Mary Magdalene was the first person to whom the risen Jesus appeared.[32]

In the same chapter, Madeleine has made what I think is one of her strongest statements about the treatment of women:

> Women have been denigrated and put down by the masculine world, kept in their "proper places," whatever those were.[33]

She believes, however, that this attitude is gradually changing, and we are coming to understand the historical Jesus was ahead of his time in his treatment of women. She also suggests that, as we recognize more and more that male and female are both created in the image of God, not only will our image of ourselves change but so will our image of God. And, as always, she reminds us that this does not change God—only our perception of God.[334]

Through the vehicle of story, Madeleine L'Engle has left the indelible mark of her concern for gender equality and social justice. The thousands of letters she receives annually from children and adults, telling her they identify with her characters and are inspired by her stories, bear witness to the fact that Madeleine is a profound consciousness-raiser who has heightened our sensitivity about what it means to be a genuinely whole human being.

CHAPTER IX

Madeleine, the Mystic

For the happy ending is intrinsic to the life of faith,
central to all we do during all of our lives.
If we cannot believe in it, we are desolate indeed.
If we know, in the depths of our hearts,
that God is going to succeed,
with each one of us, with the entire universe,
then our lives will be bright with laughter, love, and light.[1]

After a lecture I once gave about Madeleine's spiritual beliefs and vision, a woman asked me, "Do you think Madeleine L'Engle is a mystic?" Her question took me by surprise, and I have thought about it often in the process of writing this book. Now, I would answer this question with an unequivocal yes.

Although there is no universally accepted definition of mysticism, there are some generally agreed-upon characteristics. A mystic is traditionally described as one who experiences in a direct way the ineffability, the unutterable nature, of divinity. Commonly acknowledged characteristics of a mystical life include a disciplined devotional practice, a commitment to prayer and contemplation, and out-of-time, or "mystical," experiences.

These characteristics are certainly true of Madeleine. Her devotional life is disciplined and rich. Her pattern of prayer and Scripture reading are clear: For more than fifty years she has drawn apart every morning and every evening to read the Bible, along with writings of church leaders and recognized saints, and to focus on God in listening prayer. She has taken spiritual nourishment from the hundreds of times she has read the Psalms and the scores of times she has read through the Bible from Genesis to Revelation.

Madeleine approaches her prayer life with similar constancy and discipline, repeating the Lord's Prayer frequently during the day. She finds it vital to pray even when she does not feel like doing so:

> If I pray only when I feel like it, God may not choose to speak. The greatest moments of prayer come in the midst of fumbling and faltering prayer, rather than the odd moment when one decides to try to turn to God.[2]

Madeleine acknowledges the importance of repetitive prayer, which she calls a contemplative mantra. In *And It Was Good,* she shares with readers the ancient "Jesus Prayer" that was suggested by her spiritual director, Canon West decades ago, and to which she has often turned:

> "Lord Jesus Christ, Son of the Living God, have mercy on me, a sinner."[3]

This prayer, she writes, "repeats itself within me"[4] . . . "like a little brook or fountain."[5] She sees the purpose of such a mantra as

> discovery of God and by God. We seek God not in order to find but to be found. When God discovers me in the deepest depths then I am truly Named, and rather than ceasing to be, I *become.*[6]

Writing, for Madeleine, is also a form of contemplative prayer, as she has described in *Walking on Water*:

> To serve a work of art is almost identical with adoring the Master of the Universe in contemplative prayer. In contemplative prayer the saint (who knows himself to be sinner, for none of us is whole, healed and holy twenty-four hours a day) turns inwards in what is called "the prayer of the heart," not to find self, but to lose self in order to be found.[7]

Madeleine understands all forms of prayer, whether written or spoken, to involve a discipline of listening:

> To pray is to listen also, to move through my own chattering to God, to that place where I can be silent and listen to what God may have to say.[8]

When Madeleine L'Engle is caught in what she calls the "overdrive" of writing, she experiences this as contemplation of the Author of the Universe, listening to God. Her stories—fiction, fantasy, and autobiographical—reflect the One she has contemplated during the act of writing.

She tells this story about the writing of her novel *The Arm of the Starfish*: She was half finished writing the book when a new character, Joshua Archer, suddenly appeared, much to her surprise. Joshua, it turns out, saves the main character's (Adam's) life and loses his own in the process. When Madeleine read the manuscript of this story to her children, they asked her to keep Joshua alive. She said she could not do this because "that's what happened."[9] (It is interesting to note that the name Joshua means "God saves" and is also another name for Jesus.)

Madeleine insists that the idea of Joshua was not hers, but was inspired by the Holy Spirit. She is a Trinitarian who believes in a God who can be known and experienced in three forms. In *The Irrational Season*, she states that, for her, the Holy Spirit, the third aspect of the Trinity, is "the easiest of this not-at-all-easy concept" to understand.[10]

Madeleine believes those moments during her writing when something more than herself "takes over" are the workings of the Holy Spirit.[11] One piece of evidence for this, she states, is the fact that her stories appear to "know" more than she knows. It has often happened that, years after a book is published, a reader points out a rich and beautiful meaning that Madeleine had not seen while she was writing it. A poem she wrote about the Spirit in *The Irrational Season* conveys a sense of this mystical inspiration:

> Whence comes this rush of wind?
> I stand at the earth's rim
> and feel it streaming by
> my hair, my eyes, my lips.
> I shall be blown clean off. . . .
>
> I am not here   nor there
> but caught in this great breath.
> Its rhythm cracks my ribs.
> Blown out   I am expelled
> Breathed in   I am inspired.[12]

In addition to her private devotional life, Madeleine takes time for silent retreats and looks to the Eucharist for spiritual nourishment. The celebration of communion clearly has mystical significance for her. Her poem "At Communion," from *The Weather of the Heart*, depicts something of her experience of mystery and wonder within the familiar liturgy:

> Whether I kneel or stand or sit in prayer
> I am not caught in time nor held in space,
> But thrust beyond this posture, I am where
> Time and eternity are face to face;
> Infinity and space meet in this place
> Where crossbar and upright hold the One
> In agony and in all Love's embrace.
> The power in helplessness which was begun
> When all the brilliance of the flaming sun

Contained itself in the small confines of a child
Now comes to me in this strange action done
In mystery. Break time, break space, O wild
And lovely power. Break me: thus am I dead,
Am resurrected now in wine and bread.[13]

Madeleine shares from her own spiritual journey in *Bright Evening Star*, telling about her exposure to religion and religious practices as a child. She reveals, very simply, the following profound mystical experience she experienced as a child:

> One day I was in the bathroom, standing at the basin, washing my hands. And Jesus was there. In the bathroom with me. Telling me without words that it was all right and there was work for me to do. I did not question his presence. It seemed very strange and embarrassing to me that he would approach me in the bathroom, because I was a private and rather prudish child.[14]

Until she wrote this in *Bright Evening Star*, Madeleine says,

> Certainly I didn't tell anybody. I have never mentioned it before in all these years. But I didn't forget.[15]

Perhaps this first mystical experience, this moment of revelation, became a touchstone along the way for Madeleine. While many of her questions, then and now, remain unanswered, she accepts and recognizes a dimension to reality that she calls "mystery."[16]

Madeleine describes another mystical experience in *The Summer of the Great-grandmother*. She had flown to England to visit her daughter, Josephine; her son-in-law, Alan Jones; and her two baby granddaughters, Léna and Charlotte. Riding from the airport in the Jones' small car, with Charlotte on her lap, she and Josephine began singing to the children. Madeleine was hungry and weary from the trip. She writes,

> Suddenly, the world unfolded, and I moved into an indescribable place of many dimensions where colors were more bril-

liant and more varied than those of the everyday world. The unfolding continued; everything deepened and opened, and I glimpsed relationships in which the truth of love was fully revealed.[17]

Madeleine describes this experience as "ineffably glorious" but also frightening because she had to return "to the self which was still singing to the sleeping baby." She knew she had to come back "from the radiance."[18]

At the core of almost all mystical experiences can be found a common thread: a genuine relationship with God. The noted church historian Georgia Harkness, in her book *Mysticism: Its Meaning and Message*, sees mysticism as essentially an experience of communion with God.[19] The evidence of Madeleine L'Engle's deep communion with God is sprinkled throughout her stories, poems, and prayers. She has a relationship with a God of love, a God beyond human knowing who can be understood only with the heart, a God she believes lives both within the human soul and out among the stars and galaxies. Love, the supreme identifying characteristic of an encounter with the divine, is the last word in everything Madeleine writes. The God she believes in and seeks to serve is a God who persists in love

> until we can all, all of us without exception, freely return his look of love with love in our own eyes and hearts. And then, healed, whole, complete but not finished, we will know the joy of being co-creators with the one to whom we call.[20]

Ultimately, Madeleine views our human ability to love as the key to our yet unrevealed futures:

> When we are once more known for our love, we will be the hope of the world, and we will bear the light.[21]

Yet she does not suggest that this love is so mysterious we cannot attain it. In the Incarnation of the Christ, Madeleine sees the possibility that, as fallible human beings, we can know our woundedness, yet know we are loved by God:

> Our love of God, and God's love for us, is most often expressed in dailiness. The incarnation is an affirmation of the value and richness of dailiness, and of the rhythm of work and play.[22]

Georgia Harkness also suggests that communion with God includes affirmation of our human selves.[23] Madeleine's concept of "naming" (which she popularized, if she did not invent it) is rooted in this intimate knowing. In *A Wind in the Door,* the cherubim Proginoskes explains to Meg Murry that a Namer is one who helps the who-or-what being named to be "more particularly" the person or thing he-she-it is "supposed to be."[24] This echoes Madeleine's belief that only when we know ourselves to be "named" can we know we are accepted and loved as we are. And only when we are in that space created by love and acceptance can we become fully ourselves. As Proginoskes claims,

> "That('s) what makes persons know who they are."[25]

Part of Madeleine's spiritual life is her passion to "live fully as a woman."[26] This parallels what Parker Palmer has suggested in his book *The Active Life,* that "the heart of the spiritual quest is to know 'the rapture of being alive.' "[27] It is obvious that Madeleine experiences herself most fully, is most alive, in her writing:

> In story I recognize my own humanness, and the call to become more fully human—not perfect, but human—bearing within me the image of my Maker.[28]

In his book *Discovering God Within,* Quaker spiritual director John R. Yungblut writes of the "extroverted mystic"—an individual, such as an artist, who sees himself or herself as a part of a larger whole. This is congruent with the posture of pacifism and nonviolence that characterizes the mystic who perceives reality in terms of "unity, relatedness, [and] wholeness."[29] Palmer concurs that mystics experience a sense of identity and connectedness with all human beings; they are "celebrants, advocates, defenders of life."[30]

Again and again in her writing, Madeleine L'Engle portrays a similar view of the wholeness and intimate interconnectedness of the universe: from her retelling of the astrophysicists' concept of "the butterfly effect" to her poignant family dinner conversations; from her essentially pacifist views about war to her support of the equality of all people regardless of race or gender; from her care for nature to her concern about carelessness with the environment; and from her abhorrence of labels of any kind to her ecumenical view that we are all part of one family as God's children. Perhaps Madeleine's belief in the oneness of all is best expressed in *Walking on Water:*

> Artist and saint alike grope in awe to comprehend the incomprehensible disproportion of the glory of God and the humility of the Incarnation; the Master of the Universe, become of the earth, earthy, in order to be one with his creatures, so that we may be one with him.[31]

These characteristics—Madeleine's contemplative prayer, her communion with God, her sense of the interconnectedness and supreme worth of all things—together portray a deeply spiritual person. I would suggest, in Madeleine's case, these are the marks of a mystic.

Madeleine possesses another quality that Harkness identifies in the experience of the mystic: that of a spiritual vision.

> In short, mystical experience adds to the subject's grasp of reality by an intuitive rather than a logical approach. It is not by sensory experience, scientific verification, or logical deduction that the mystic's knowledge is deepened, but by a clearer vision and a depth of feeling that seem to come from a Source beyond himself. This is why in Christian mysticism so strong an emphasis is laid on the love of God.[32]

Madeleine's own thought-provoking definition of a mystic parallels this trust in knowledge from "a Source beyond":

> A mystic is a person who sees the facts as inadequate.[33]

For Madeleine, there is always more to know than "the facts." Because she believes that story can go where facts cannot take us, she uses fiction to help us move to that "beyond place" where we can find answers to questions that have no answers, identify and move through illusion, touch reality, and come to meaning and truth.[34]

In *Walking on Water,* she describes what it means for her to "go beyond":

> When I am working, I move into an area of faith which is beyond the conscious control of my intellect. I do not mean that I discard my intellect, that I am an anti-intellectual gung ho for intuition and intuition only. Like it or not, I *am* an intellectual. The challenge is to let my intellect work *for* the creative act, not against it.[35]

For Madeleine, being an artist means letting go of control and surrendering herself completely and absolutely to the Creator God she seeks to serve through her writing. This posture of faith allows her to "listen" for her stories.

As she writes, Madeleine is true to her vocation as a co-creator with God, observing and contemplating the Creation. As she shapes her ideas about God, the cosmos, and human existence into story form, her symbols, images, metaphors, and stories convey her spiritual vision.

I experienced this firsthand a few summers ago when I was one of thirty or so people who gathered for a two-week event in creative writing led by Madeleine. She met us with contagious acceptance, appreciation, and warmth. The love visible in her written words was equally apparent in her person. The rainbow of Light, in which she experiences the mysterious, the numinous, the miraculous in the ordinary things of daily life, was reflected as she led us to write with passion and authenticity. Fired by her encouragement to "listen" to our imaginations and hearts and the Source beyond, we were "named" and provided with a context in which we could become the Namers of others.

Madeleine's love of words, and her mystical relationship with the Word, have been expressed most eloquently in the poem with which she opens the ninth chapter of *Penguins and Golden Calves*:

> Word
> I, who live by words, am wordless when
> I try my words in prayer. All language turns
> To silence. Prayer will take my words and then
> Reveal their emptiness. The stilled voice learns
> To hold its peace, to listen with the heart
> To silence that is joy, is adoration.
> The self is shattered, all words torn apart
> In this strange patterned time of
>   contemplation
> That, in time breaks time, breaks words,
>   breaks me,
> And then, in silence, leaves me healed and
>   mended.
> I leave, return to language, for I see
> Through words, even when all words are
>   ended.
> I, who live by words, am wordless when
> I turn me to the Word to pray. Amen.[36]

Madeleine L'Engle's true gift, offered through her mystical vocation of listening and writing—and born of this contemplative prayer—is the gift of "making visible." Her writings are like suncatchers that, when suspended in the sunlight of our lives, translate the invisible light of the *mysterium tremendum* into a many faceted rainbow that becomes visible in the living space of our hearts and minds. In that rainbow, we can find affirmation and new meaning and healing for our life's journey.

APPENDICES

APPENDIX A
Books by Madeleine L'Engle

An Acceptable Time. New York: Farrar, Straus & Giroux, 1989; New York: Dell Publishing, 1990.

And Both Were Young. New York: Delacorte Press, 1949; New York: Lothrop, 1949; New York: Dell Publishing, 1983.

And It Was Good: Reflections on Beginnings. Wheaton, IL: Harold Shaw Publishers, 1983.

The Anti-Muffins. Illustrated by Gloria Ortiz. New York: Pilgrim Press, 1980.

Anytime Prayers. Photos by Maria Rooney. Wheaton, IL: Harold Shaw Publishers, 1994.

The Arm of the Starfish. New York: Farrar, Straus & Giroux, 1965; New York: Dell Publishing, 1980.

Bright Evening Star: Mystery of the Incarnation. Wheaton, IL: Harold Shaw Publishers, 1997.

Camilla Dickinson. New York: Simon & Schuster, 1951. Reissued as *Camilla*. New York: Crowell, 1965; New York: Delacorte Press, 1981; New York: Dell Publishing, 1982.

Certain Women. New York: Farrar, Straus & Giroux, 1992; San Francisco: Harper and Row, 1993.

A Circle of Quiet. New York: Farrar, Straus & Giroux, 1972; San Francisco: Harper and Row, 1977.

A Cry Like a Bell. Wheaton, IL: Harold Shaw Publishers, 1987.

Dance in the Desert. Illustrated by Symeon Shimin. New York: Farrar, Straus & Giroux, 1969.

Dragons in the Waters. New York: Farrar, Straus & Giroux, 1976; New York: Dell Publishing, 1982.

18 Washington Square, South: A Comedy in One Act. Boston and Los Angeles: Baker's Plays, 1944.

Everyday Prayers. Illustrated by Lucile Butel. New York: Morehouse-Barlow, 1974.

Friends for the Journey. With Luci Shaw. Ann Arbor, MI: Servant Publications, 1997.

Glimpses of Grace: Daily Thoughts and Reflections. Edited by Carole F. Chase. San Francisco: HarperCollins, 1996.

The Glorious Impossible. New York: Simon and Schuster, 1990.

A House Like a Lotus. New York: Farrar, Straus & Giroux, 1984; New York: Dell Publishing, 1985.

Ilsa. New York: Vanguard Press, 1946.

The Irrational Season. New York: Seabury Press, 1977; San Francisco: Harper and Row, 1983; New York: Farrar, Straus & Giroux, 1987.

The Journey with Jonah. Illustrated by Leonard Everett Fisher. New York: Farrar, Straus & Giroux, 1967; reissued, 1991.

Ladder of Angels. San Francisco: Harper and Row, 1979; New York: Penguin, 1980.

Lines Scribbled on an Envelope. New York: Farrar, Straus & Giroux, 1969.

A Live Coal in the Sea. New York: Farrar, Straus & Giroux, 1996.

The Love Letters. New York: Farrar, Straus & Giroux, 1966; New York: Ballantine Books, 1983. Revised edition, Wheaton, IL: Harold Shaw Publishers, 1997.

Many Waters. New York: Farrar, Straus & Giroux, 1986; New York: Dell Publishing, 1987.

Meet the Austins. New York: Vanguard Press, 1960; New York: Dell Publishing, 1981; New York: Farrar, Straus & Giroux, 1997. (This edition includes a chapter originally published as *The Anti-Muffins*.)

The Moon by Night. New York: Farrar, Straus & Giroux, 1963; New York: Dell Publishing, 1981.

Moses, Prince of Egypt. New York: Puffin Books, 1998.

Mothers & Daughters. Photos by Maria Rooney. Wheaton, IL: Harold Shaw Publishers, 1997.

The Other Side of the Sun. New York: Farrar, Straus & Giroux, 1971; New York: Bantam Books, 1972; New York: Ballantine Books, 1983; Wheaton, IL: Harold Shaw Publishers, 1996.

Penguins and Golden Calves: Icons and Idols. Wheaton, IL: Harold Shaw Publishers, 1996.

Prayers for Sunday. New York: Morehouse-Barlow, 1974.

A Ring of Endless Light. New York: Farrar, Straus & Giroux, 1980; New York: Dell Publishing, 1981.

The Rock That Is Higher: Story as Truth. Wheaton, IL: Harold Shaw Publishers, 1993.

A Severed Wasp. New York: Farrar, Straus & Giroux, 1982.

The Small Rain. New York: Vanguard Press, 1945; New York: Farrar, Straus & Giroux, 1984. First section reissued as *Prelude*, New York: Vanguard Press, 1968.

Sold into Egypt: Joseph's Journey into Human Being. Wheaton, IL: Harold Shaw Publishers, 1989.

The Sphinx at Dawn. San Francisco: Harper and Row, 1982.

A Stone for a Pillow: Journeys with Jacob. Wheaton, IL: Harold Shaw Publishers, 1986.

The Summer of the Great-grandmother. New York: Farrar, Straus & Giroux, 1974.

A Swiftly Tilting Planet. New York: Farrar, Straus & Giroux, 1978; New York: Dell Publishing, 1979.

Trailing Clouds of Glory: Spiritual Values in Children's Literature. Edited with Avery Brooke. Philadelphia: Westminster Press, 1985.

Troubling a Star. New York: Farrar, Straus & Giroux, 1994; Dell Publishing, 1995.

The Twenty-Four Days Before Christmas. New York: Farrar, Straus & Giroux, 1964; Wheaton, IL: Harold Shaw Publishers, 1984, Illustrated by Joe de Velasco.

Two-Part Invention: The Story of a Marriage. New York: Farrar, Straus & Giroux, 1988; San Francisco: Harper and Row, 1989.

Walking on Water: Reflections on Faith and Art. Wheaton, IL: Harold Shaw Publishers, 1980; New York: Farrar, Straus & Giroux, 1995; Wheaton, Il: Harold Shaw Publishers, 1998, Commemorative edition in honor of Madeleine's 80th birthday.

The Weather of the Heart. Wheaton, IL: Harold Shaw Publishers, 1978.

A Wind in the Door. New York: Farrar, Straus & Giroux, 1973; New York: Dell Publishing, 1976.

A Winter's Love. Philadelphia: Lippincott, 1957; New York: Ballantine Books, 1983.

Winter Song: Christmas Readings by Madeleine L'Engle & Luci Shaw. With Luci Shaw. Wheaton, IL: Harold Shaw Publishers, 1996.

A Wrinkle in Time. New York: Farrar, Straus & Giroux, 1962; New York: Dell Publishing, 1976.

The Young Unicorns. New York: Farrar, Straus & Giroux, 1968; New York: Dell Publishing, 1980.

OTHER BOOKS ABOUT MADELEINE L'ENGLE

Gonzales, Doreen. *Madeleine L'Engle: Author of a Wrinkle in Time.* New York: Dillon Press, 1991.

Hettinga, Donald R. *Presenting Madeleine L'Engle.* New York: Twayne Publishers, 1993.

The Swiftly Tilting Worlds of Madeleine L'Engle. Edited by Luci Shaw. Wheaton, IL: Harold Shaw Publishers, 1998.

APPENDIX B
The Structure of the L'Engle Corpus

ADULT FICTION
The Small Rain, 1945
Ilsa, 1946
Camilla Dickinson, 1951 (reissued as *Camilla*, 1965)
A Winter's Love, 1957
The Love Letters, 1966
The Other Side of the Sun, 1971
A Severed Wasp, 1982
Certain Women, 1992
A Live Coal in the Sea, 1996

YOUNG ADULT FICTION
And Both Were Young, 1949
Meet the Austins, 1960
The Moon by Night, 1963
The Arm of the Starfish, 1965
The Young Unicorns, 1968
Dragons in the Waters, 1976
A Ring of Endless Light, 1980
A House Like a Lotus, 1984
Troubling a Star, 1994

* Note: *The categories and the placement of titles within them are my own. I take full responsibility for both.—Carole F. Chase*

FANTASY
The Time Trilogy:
    A Wrinkle in Time, 1962
    A Wind in the Door, 1973
    A Swiftly Tilting Planet, 1978
Dance in the Desert, 1969
The Sphinx at Dawn, 1982
Many Waters, 1986
An Acceptable Time, 1989

AUTOBIOGRAPHICAL
Crosswicks Journals:
    A Circle of Quiet, 1972
    The Summer of the Great-grandmother, 1974
    The Irrational Season, 1977
    Two-Part Invention: The Story of a Marriage, 1988

PERSONAL REFLECTIONS ON SCRIPTURE
The Journey with Jonah (a play), 1967, 1991
Ladder of Angels, 1979
Genesis Trilogy:
    And It Was Good: Reflections on Beginnings, 1983
    A Stone for a Pillow: Journeys with Jacob, 1986
    Sold into Egypt: Joseph's Journey into Human Being, 1989
The Glorious Impossible, 1990
The Rock That Is Higher: Story as Truth, 1993
Penguins and Golden Calves: Icons and Idols, 1996
Bright Evening Star, 1997

CHILDREN'S BOOKS
The Twenty-Four Days Before Christmas, 1964
The Anti-Muffins, 1980 (also included in the 1997 edition of *Meet the Austins*
    published by Farrar, Straus & Giroux)
Moses, Prince of Egypt, 1998

PRAYERS
Everyday Prayers, 1974
Prayers for Sunday, 1974
Anytime Prayers, with photos by Maria Rooney, 1994
Mothers and Daughters, with photos by Maria Rooney, 1997

POETRY

Lines Scribbled on an Envelope, 1969
The Weather of the Heart, 1978
A Cry Like a Bell, 1987

SPECIAL BOOKS

18 Washington Square, South: A Comedy in One Act, 1944
Walking on Water: Reflections on Faith and Art, 1980
Trailing Clouds of Glory: Spiritual Values in Children's Literature, with Avery
    Brooke, 1985
Winter Song: Christmas Readings by Madeleine L'Engle and Luci Shaw, 1996
Glimpses of Grace: Daily Thoughts and Reflections, edited by Carole Chase, 1996
Friends for the Journey, with Luci Shaw, 1997

APPENDIX C

A Chronology of Madeleine L'Engle's Life and Books

1918	Madeleine L'Engle Camp is born on November 29 in New York City.
1929	The Camps moves to a Chateau in the French Alps; Madeleine attends boarding school in Switzerland.
1933	Returns to the United States; lives in northern Florida. Attends Ashley Hall, a boarding school in Charleston, South Carolina.
1935	Madeleine's father, Charles Camp, dies.
1937	Madeleine enrolls in Smith College.
1941	Graduates from Smith; moves to an apartment in New York.
1942	Plays role in *The Cherry Orchard*; meets Hugh Franklin.

LIFE EVENTS

PUBLICATIONS

	LIFE EVENTS		PUBLICATIONS
		1945	• *The Small Rain*
1946	• Marries Hugh Franklin on January 26.	1946	• *Ilsa*
	• The couple buys Crosswicks.		
1947	• Daughter Josephine is born.		
		1949	• *And Both Were Young*
		1951	• *Camilla Dickinson*
1952	• Madeleine, Hugh, and Josephine move to Crosswicks.		
	• Purchase and run a small general store.		
	• Son Bion is born.		
1956	• Maria comes to live with the Franklins.		
		1957	• *A Winter's Love*

LIFE EVENTS	PUBLICATIONS

1959 • The Franklins leave in early spring on a 10-week cross- country camping trip before moving to New York.

1960 • Begins teaching at St. Hilda's and St. Hugh's Anglican School.

1960 • *Meet the Austins*

1962 • *A Wrinkle in Time*

1963 • Wins the John Newbery Medal for *Wrinkle*.

1963 • *The Moon by Night*

1964 • *Wrinkle* is runner-up for Hans Christian Andersen Award.

1964 • *The Twenty-Four Days Before Christmas*

1965 • Begins working as volunteer librarian in Cathedral of St. John the Divine.
• Receives Sequoyah Award and Lewis Carroll Shelf Award for *Wrinkle*.

1965 • *The Arm of the Starfish*
• *Camilla* (revised)

1966 • Last year of teaching at St. Hilda's and St. Hugh's.

1966 • *The Love Letters*

1967 • *The Journey with Jonah*

1968 • *The Young Unicorns*

1969 • Wins Austrian State Literary Prize for *The Moon by Night*.

1969 • *Dance in the Desert*
• *Lines Scribbled on an Envelope*

1971 • Wins Austrian State Literary Prize for *Camilla*.
• Her mother, Madeleine Camp, dies at 90.

1971 • *The Other Side of the Sun*

1972 • Wins Order of St. John of Jerusalem. Workshop leader at University of Rochester.

1972 • *A Circle of Quiet*

1974 • Wins New England Round Table of Children's Librarian Honor Certificate.

1973 • *A Wind in the Door*

1974 • *Everyday Prayers*
• *Prayers for Sunday*
• *The Summer of the Great-grandmother*

1975 • Is invited by Clyde S. Kilby to deposit her papers and manuscripts in Special Collections part of the Buswell Library at Wheaton College in Illinois.

1976 • L'Engle collection is begun at Wheaton.

1976 • *Dragons in the Waters*

1977 • Granddaughter Léna Jones hit by a truck on July 13 and survives.

1977 • *The Irrational Season*

1978 • Wins Learning A-V Award for *A Wind in the Door*.
• Wins University of Southern Mississippi Medallion.
• *The Irrational Season* is named the Seabury Lenten Selection.

1978 • *The Weather of the Heart*
• *A Swiftly Tilting Planet*

LIFE EVENTS

1979 • Wins the National Religious Book Award for *The Weather of the Heart.*

1980 • *A Ring of Endless Light* is named a Newbery Honor Book.
• Wins American Book Award for *A Swiftly Tilting Planet.*
• Wins National Religious Book Award for *Ladder of Angels.*
• Awarded honorary Doctor of Letters degree from Gordon College.

1981 • Receives Dorothy Canfield Fisher Children's Book Award for *A Ring of Endless Light,* which is also nominated for a Newbery Medal.
• Receives Smith College Award for service to community or college which exemplifies the purposes of liberal arts education.
• Receives Newbery Honor Award for *A Swiftly Tilting Planet.*

1982 • Awarded the California Young Reader Medal for *A Ring of Endless Light.*
• Receives honorary Doctorate of Humane Letters from the Christian Theological Seminary in Indianapolis.
• Is made an honorary citizen of Louisville, Kentucky.

1983 • Receives the Colorado Children's Book Award for *A Ring of Endless Light.*
• Receives Honorary Doctor of Letters from Miami University, Oxford, Ohio.

1984 • Receives honorary Doctorate of Sacred Theology at the Berkeley Divinity School; Smith College Sophia Award for distinction in her field; and honorary Doctor of Literature from Wheaton College.

PUBLICATIONS

1979 • *Ladder of Angels*

1980 • *The Anti-Muffins*
• *A Ring of Endless Light*
• *Walking on Water*

1982 • *A Severed Wasp*
• *The Sphinx at Dawn*

1983 • *And It Was Good*
• *And Both Were Young* (revised)

1984 • *A House Like a Lotus*

LIFE EVENTS

1985 • Receives the Regina Medal.
• Makes a tape for Voice of America and speaks at the Library of Congress.
• Begins 2-year term as president of the Authors Guild.

1986 • Receives honorary Doctor of Letters degree from Smith College; Doctor of Humane Letters from Virginia Theological Seminary.
• Receives Weisenberg School Book Award; ALAN Award for outstanding contribution to adolescent literature from the National Council of Teachers of English.
• Trips with Hugh to Virgin Islands and China.
• Hugh dies on September 26.

1987 • Awarded honorary degree by Saint Joseph's College in West Hartford, Connecticut.

1989 • Commencement speaker at Manhattanville College, Purchase, New York; awarded an honorary Doctor of Humane Letters.

1990 • Receives the Kerlan Award. Speaks to church women in Japan in January.
• Travels to the Soviet Union in August.
• Canon West dies.

1991 • Awarded honorary Doctor of Literature by Linfield College in McMinnville, Oregon.
• Severely injured in an automobile accident in San Diego in July.

1992 • Visits Antarctica with son Bion and daughter-in-law Laurie.

1994 • Awarded Doctor of Humane Letters by Trinity College, Hartford, Connecticut, and University of the South, Sewanee, Tennessee.

PUBLICATIONS

1985 • *Trailing Clouds of Glory*

1986 • *A Stone for a Pillow*
• *Many Waters*

1987 • *A Cry Like a Bell*
• *Reading Together* (audiocassette of Madeleine and Hugh)

1988 • *Two-Part Invention*

1989 • *Sold into Egypt*
• *An Acceptable Time*

1990 • *The Glorious Impossible*

1992 • *Certain Women*

1993 • *The Rock That Is Higher*
• audiocassette of *A Wrinkle in Time*

1994 • *Troubling a Star*
• audiocassette of *A Wind in the Door*
• *Anytime Prayers*

LIFE EVENTS

1995
- Writer-in-residence for *Victoria* magazine.
- Trip to Ireland for conference on myth at Trinity College, Dublin; travels in Scotland, London.
- Talks at Santa Cruz University and New College at Berkeley.

1996
- Corrective foot/ankle surgery.
- Writers workshop in British Columbia.
- Crosswicks Cottage refurbished for Connecticut living.
- Honorary degrees in Humane Letters, Elon College, North Carolina, and the University of Rhode Island.

1997
- Women's Lectureship, Fuller Theological Seminary.

1998
- In honor of her 80th birthday, Harold Shaw Publishers presented Madeleine with a *Festschrift* written by her friends and edited by Luci Shaw entitled *The Swiftly Tilting Worlds of Madeleine L'Engle*.
- Awarded the Margaret A. Edwards Award for lifetime writing for teens.
- Faculty member at the International Centennial Celebration of C.S. Lewis held at Oxford and Cambridge, England.

PUBLICATIONS

1995
- Audiocassette of *Two-Part Invention*

1996
- *Glimpses of Grace*, with Carole Chase
- *Penguins and Golden Calves*
- *A Live Coal in the Sea*
- *A Winter's Song*, with Luci Shaw
- Audiocassette of *A Swiftly Tilting Planet*

1997
- *Mothers and Daughters*
- *Bright Evening Star*
- *Friends for the Journey*, with Luci Shaw

1998
- *Moses, Prince of Egypt*

APPENDIX D
Madeleine L'Engle's Newbery Medal Award Speech

"The Expanding Universe"

Newbery Medal award speech given by Madeleine L'Engle at the meeting of the American Library Association in Chicago, July 15, 1963. The Newbery Medal for "the most distinguished contribution to American literature for children" was awarded to Madeleine for A Wrinkle in Time.

For a writer of fiction to have to sit down and write a speech, especially a speech in which she must try to express her gratitude for one of the greatest honors of her life, is as difficult a task as she can face. She can no longer hide behind the printed page and let her characters speak for her; she must stand up in front of an illustrious group of librarians, editors, publishers, writers, feeling naked, the way one sometimes does in a dream. What, then, does she say? Should she merely tell a series of anecdotes about her life and how she happened to write this book? Or should she try to be profound and write a speech that will go down in the pages of history, comparable only to the Gettysburg Address? Should she stick to platitudes that will offend no one and say nothing? Perhaps she tries all of these several times and then tears them up, knowing that if she doesn't her husband will do it for her, and decides simply to say some of the things she feels deeply about.

I can't tell you anything about children's books that you don't already know. I'm not teaching you; you're teaching me. All I can tell you is how Ruth Gagliardo's telephone call about the Newbery Medal has affected me over the past few months.

One of my greatest treasures is the letter Mr. Melcher wrote me, one of the last letters he wrote, talking about the medal and saying he had just read *A Wrinkle in Time* and had been excited about it. This was one of the qualities that made him what he was: the ability to be excited. Bertha Mahony Miller in her article "Frederic G. Melcher—A Twentieth Century John Newbery," says that "The bookstore's stock in trade is . . . explosive material, capable of stirring up fresh life endlessly . . . " I like here to think of another Fred, the eminent British scientist, Fred Hoyle, and his theory of the universe, in which matter is continuously being created, with the universe expanding but not dissipating. As island galaxies rush away from each other into eternity, new clouds of gas are condensing into new galaxies. As old stars die, new stars are being born. Mr. Melcher lived in this universe of continuous creation and expansion. It would be impossible to overestimate his influence on books, particularly children's books; impossible to overestimate his influence on the people who read books, write them, sell them, get enthusiastic about them. We are all here tonight because of his vision, and we would be less than fair to his memory if we didn't resolve to keep alive his excitement and his ability to grow, to change, to expand.

I am of the first generation to profit by Mr. Melcher's excitement, having been born shortly before he established the Newbery award, and growing up with most of these books on my shelves. I learned about mankind from Hendrik Willem van Loon; I traveled with Dr. Dolittle, created by a man I called Hug Lofting; Will James taught me about the West with Smoky; in boarding school I grabbed *Invincible Louisa* the moment it came into the library because Louisa May Alcott had the same birthday that I have, and the same ambitions. And now to be a very small link in the long chain of these writers, of the men and women who led me into the expanding universe, is both an honor and a responsibility. It is an honor for which I am deeply grateful to Mr. Melcher and to those of you who decided *A Wrinkle in Time* was worthy of it.

The responsibility has caused me to think seriously during these past months on the subject of vocation, the responsibility added to the fact that I'm working now on a movie scenario about a Portuguese nun who lived in the mid-1600's had no vocation, was seduced and then betrayed by a French soldier of fortune, and, in the end, through suffering, came into a true vocation. I believe that every one of us here tonight has as clear and vital a vocation as anyone in a religious order. We have the vocation of keeping alive Mr. Melcher's excitement in leading young people into an expanding imagination. Because of the very nature of the world as it is today our children receive in school a heavy load of scientific and analytical subjects, so it is in their reading for fun, for pleasure, that they must be guided into creativity. There are forces working in the world as never before in the history of mankind for standardization, for the regimentation of us all, or what I like to call making muffins of us, muffins all like every other muffin in the muffin tin. This is the limited universe, the dying, dissipating universe, that we can help our children avoid by providing them with "explosive material capable of stirring up fresh life endlessly."

So how do we do it? We can't just sit down at our typewriters and turn out explosive material. I took a course in college on Chaucer, one of the most explosive, imaginative, and far-reaching in influence of all writers. And I'll never forget going to the final exam and being asked why Chaucer used certain verbal devices, certain adjectives, why he had certain characters behave in certain ways. And I wrote in a white heat of fury, "I don't think Chaucer had any idea why he did any of these things. That isn't the way people write."

I believe this as strongly now as I did then. Most of what is best in writing isn't done deliberately.

Do I mean, then, that an author should sit around like a phony Zen Buddhist in his pad, drinking endless cups of espresso coffee and waiting for inspiration to descend upon him? That isn't the way the writer works, either. I heard a famous author say once that the hardest part of writing a book was making yourself sit down at the typewriter. I know what he meant. Unless a writer works constantly to improve and refine the tools of his trade, they will be useless instruments if and when the moment of inspiration, of revelation, does come. This is the moment when a writer is spoken through, the moment that a writer must accept with gratitude and humility, and then attempt, as best he can, to communicate to others.

A writer of fantasy, fairy tale, or myth must inevitable discover that he is not writing out of his own knowledge or experience, but out of something both deeper and wider. I think that fantasy must possess the author and simply use him. I know that this is true of *A Wrinkle in Time*. I can't possibly tell you how I came to write it. It was simply a book I had to write. I had no choice. And it was only *after* it was written that I realized what some of it meant.

Very few children have any problem with the world of the imagination; it's their own world, the world of their daily life, and it's our loss that so many of us grow out of it. Probably this group here tonight is the least grown-out-of-it group that could be gathered together in one place, simply by the nature of our work. We, too, can understand how Alice could walk through the mirror into the country on the other side; how often have our children almost done this themselves? And we all understand princesses, of course. Haven't we all been badly bruised by peas? And what about the princess who spat forth toads and snakes whenever she opened her mouth to speak, and the other whose lips issued forth pieces of pure gold? We all have had days when everything we've said has seemed to turn to toads. The days of gold, alas, don't come nearly as often.

What a child doesn't realize until he is grown is that in responding to fantasy, fairy tale, and myth he is responding to what

Erich Fromm calls the one universal language, the one and only language in the world that cuts across all barriers of time, place, race, and culture. Many Newbery books are from this realm, beginning with Dr. Dolittle; books on Hindu myth, Chinese folklore, the life of Buddha, tales of American Indians, books that lead our children beyond all boundaries and into the one language of all mankind.

In the beginning God created the heaven and the earth . . . The extraordinary, the marvelous thing about Genesis is not how unscientific it is, but how amazingly accurate it is. How could the ancient Israelites have known the exact order of an evolution that wasn't to be formulated for thousands of years? Here is a truth that cuts across barriers of time and space.

But almost all of the best children's books do this, not only an *Alice in Wonderland*, a *Wind in the Willows*, a *Princess and the Goblin*. Even the most straightforward tales say far more than they seem to mean on the surface. *Little Women, The Secret Garden, Huckleberry Finn*—how much more there is in them than we realize at a first reading. They partake of the universal language, and this is why we turn to them again and again when we are children, and still again when we have grown up.

Up on the summit of Mohawk Mountain in northwest Connecticut is a large flat rock that holds the heat of the sun long after the last of the late sunset has left the sky. We take our picnics up there and then lie on the rock and watch the stars, one pulsing slowly into the deepening blue, and then another and another and another, until the sky is full of them.

A book, too, can be a star, "explosive material, capable of stirring up fresh life endlessly," a living fire to lighten the darkness, leading out into the expanding universe.

— Madeleine L'Engle
July, 1963

APPENDIX E

Families in Madeleine L'Engle's Fiction

Key to Title Abbreviations

FICTION

ANTI-MUFFINS - *The Anti-Muffins* (1980)
ARM - *The Arm of the Starfish* (1965)
AUSTINS - *Meet the Austins* (1960)
CAMILLA - *Camilla Dickinson* (1951)
COAL - *A Live Coal in the Sea* (1996)
DANCE - *Dance in the Desert* (1969)
DAYS - *Twenty-Four Days Before Christmas* (1964)
DRAGONS - *Dragons in the Waters* (1976)
HOUSE - *A House Like a Lotus* (1984)
ILSA - *Ilsa* (1945)
JONAH - *The Journey with Jonah* (1967)
LADDER - *Ladder of Angels* (1979)
LETTERS - *The Love Letters* (1966)
LOVE - *A Winter's Love* (1957)
MOON - *The Moon by Night* (1963)
PLANET - *A Swiftly Tilting Planet* (1976)
RAIN - *The Small Rain* (1945)
RING - *A Ring of Endless Light* (1980)
SPHINX - *The Sphinx at Dawn* (1982)
SQUARE - *18 Washington Square* (1944)
STAR - *Troubling a Star* (1994)
SUN - *The Other Side of the Sun* (1971)
TIME - *An Acceptable Time* (1989)
WASP - *A Severed Wasp* (1982)
WATERS - *Many Waters* (1986)
WIND - *A Wind in the Door* (1973)
WOMEN - *Certain Women* (1992)
WRINKLE)- *A Wrinkle in Time* (1962)
UNICORNS - *The Young Unicorns* (1968)
YOUNG - *And Both Were Young* (1949)

NONFICTION

ANYTIME - *Anytime Prayers* (1994)
BELL - *A Cry Like a Bell* (1987)
BRIGHT - *Bright Evening Star* (1997)
CIRCLE - *A Circle of Quiet* (1972)
CLOUDS - *Trailing Clouds of Glory* (1985)
EVERYDAY - *Everyday Prayers* (1974)
FRIENDS - *Friends for the Journey* (1997)
GLORIOUS - *The Glorious Impossible* (1990)
GOOD - *And It Was Good* (1983)
INVENTION - *Two-Part Invention* (1988)
LADDER - *Ladder of Angels* (1979)
LINES - *Lines Scribbled on an Envelope* (1969)
MOTHERS - *Mothers and Daughters* (1997)
PENGUINS - *Penguins and Golden Calves* (1996)
PRAYERS - *Prayers for Sunday* (1974)
ROCK - *The Rock That Is Higher* (1993)
SEASON - *The Irrational Season* (1977)
SOLD - *Sold Into Egypt* (1989)
SONG - *Winter Song* (1996)
STONE - *A Stone for a Pillow* (1986)
SUMMER - *The Summer of the Great-Grandmother* (1974)
WALKING - *Walking on Water* (1980)
WEATHER - *The Weather of the Heart* (1978)

NOTE: Dates listed are for first time publication of each book.

Madeleine L'Engle's

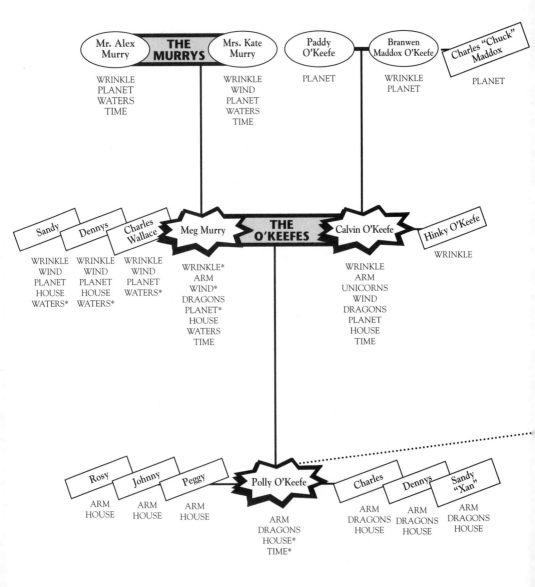

Major Families

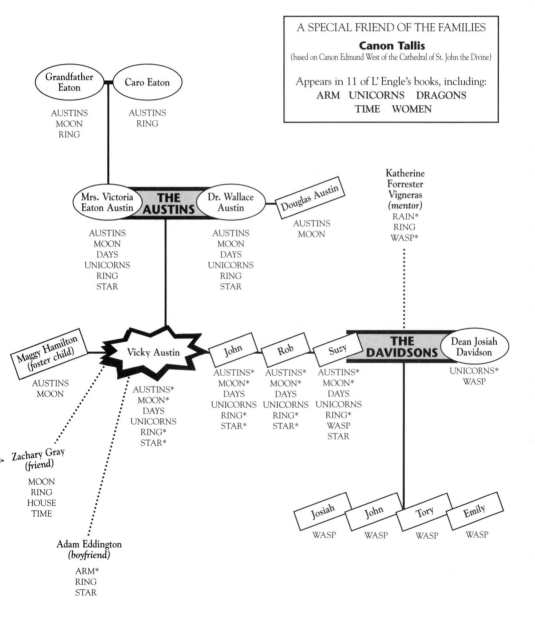

A SPECIAL FRIEND OF THE FAMILIES

Canon Tallis
(based on Canon Edmund West of the Cathedral of St. John the Divine)

Appears in 11 of L'Engle's books, including:
ARM   UNICORNS   DRAGONS
TIME   WOMEN

Grandfather Eaton
AUSTINS
MOON
RING

Caro Eaton
AUSTINS
RING

Katherine Forrester Vigneras
(mentor)
RAIN*
RING
WASP*

Mrs. Victoria Eaton Austin
AUSTINS
MOON
DAYS
UNICORNS
RING
STAR

THE AUSTINS

Dr. Wallace Austin
AUSTINS
MOON
DAYS
UNICORNS
RING
STAR

Douglas Austin
AUSTINS
MOON

Maggy Hamilton (foster child)
AUSTINS
MOON

Vicky Austin
AUSTINS*
MOON*
DAYS
UNICORNS
RING*
STAR*

John
AUSTINS*
MOON*
DAYS
UNICORNS
RING*
STAR*

Rob
AUSTINS*
MOON*
DAYS
UNICORNS
RING*
STAR*

Suzy
AUSTINS*
MOON*
DAYS
UNICORNS
RING*
WASP
STAR

THE DAVIDSONS

Dean Josiah Davidson
UNICORNS*
WASP

Zachary Gray (friend)
MOON
RING
HOUSE
TIME

Adam Eddington (boyfriend)
ARM*
RING
STAR

Josiah
WASP

John
WASP

Tory
WASP

Emily
WASP

* = *protagonist*

The David Wheaton Family

(in *Certain Women*)

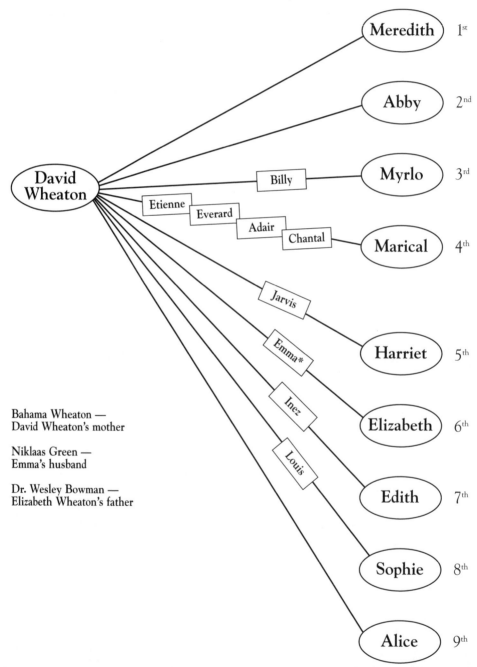

Bahama Wheaton —
David Wheaton's mother

Niklaas Green —
Emma's husband

Dr. Wesley Bowman —
Elizabeth Wheaton's father

The Dickinsons and Xanthakos Families

(in *Camilla Dickinson* and *A Live Coal in the Sea*)

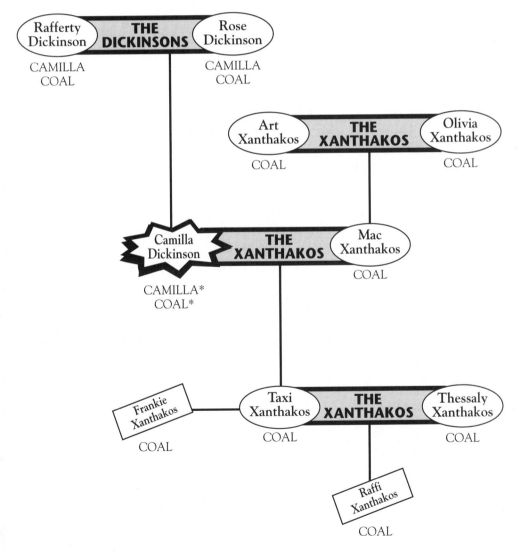

* = *protagonist*

APPENDIX F
Characters in Madeleine L'Engle's Fiction

Adnarel [a seraphim] - WATERS
Alarid [a seraphim] - WATERS
Baltazar Alcoforado - LETTERS
Marianna Alcoforado - LETTERS*
Peregrina Alcoforado - LETTERS
Anah - WATERS
Anaral - TIME
Joshua Archer - ARM
Sister Maria de Assuncao - LETTERS
Elena (Huxley) Austin - AUSTINS,
    MOON
John Austin - AUSTINS, MOON,
    DAYS, UNICORNS,
    ANTI-MUFFINS, RING,
    STAR
Rob Austin - AUSTINS, MOON,
    DAYS, UNICORNS,
    ANTI-MUFFINS, RING,
    STAR
Suzy Austin (Davidson) - AUSTINS,
    MOON, DAYS, UNICORNS,
    RING, WASP, STAR
Vicky Austin - AUSTINS,*
    MOON,* DAYS,*
    UNICORNS,
    ANTI-MUFFINS,* RING,*
    STAR*
Victoria Eaton Austin - AUSTINS,
    MOON, DAYS, UNICORNS,
    ANTI-MUFFINS, RING,
    STAR

Wallace Austin - AUSTINS,
    MOON, DAYS, UNICORNS,
    ANTI-MUFFINS, RING,
    STAR
Blajeny [a teacher] - WIND
Bishop Felix Bodeway - RAIN,
    WASP
[Court] Courtney Bowen - LOVE
Emily Bowen - LOVE*
[Vee] Virginia Bowen (Porcher) -
    LOVE, HOUSE
Connie Bowen - LOVE
The Rev. Wesley Bowman -
    WOMEN
Ilsa Brandes - ILSA
Dr. John Brandes - ILSA
Abbess Donna Brites - LETTERS
Bishop Ming Chan - WASP
James Clement - LETTERS
Dr. Louise Colubra - WRINKLE,
    WIND, TIME
Bishop Nason Colubra - TIME
Adam Cook - STAR
Seth Cook - STAR
Sarah Courtmont - RAIN
Cub - TIME
[Kali] Carolyn Cutter - ARM
Typhon Cutter - ARM
Emily Davidson - WASP
John Davidson - WASP

---

* = *protagonist*   ( ) = *maiden name*   SEE TITLE ABBREVIATION CHART PG 179

Dean [Dave} Josiah Davidson - UNICORNS,* WASP

Jos Davidson - WASP

Suzy Austin Davidson - see Suzy Austin

Tory Davidson - WASP

Camilla Dickinson (Xanthakos) - CAMILLA,* COAL*

[Raffi] Rafferty Dickinson - CAMILLA, COAL

Rose Dickinson - CAMILLA, COAL

Mademoiselle Dragonet - YOUNG

Father Duarte - LETTERS

Eagle Woman - TIME

Caro Eaton - AUSTINS, RING

Grandfather Eaton - AUSTINS, MOON, RING,

Eblis [a nephilim] - WATERS

Adam Eddington - ARM,* RING, STAR

Aunt Serena Eddington - STAR

Dr. Edith Edison - COAL

Elisheba - WATERS

Enoch - WATERS

Mother Escolastica - LETTERS

Siri Evensen - STAR

Dr. Joaquin Ferreira - LETTERS

Abe Fielding - LOVE

Sam Fielding - LOVE

Quimby Forrest - STAR

Julie Forrester - STAR

Katherine Forrester (Vigneras) - RAIN,* RING, WASP*

Thomas Forrester - RAIN

Gaudior [a unicorn] - PLANET

David Gauss - CAMILLA

Dorcas Gibson - WASP

Terry Gibson - WASP

[Fatty] Fatima Gomez - WASP

Topaze Gomez - WASP

Dr. Iona Grady - WASP

Andrew Grange - COAL

Hariet Grange - COAL

[Liz] Elizabeth Grange - COAL

Noelle Grange - COAL

[Red] Grantley Grange - COAL

Zachary Gray - MOON, RING, HOUSE, TIME

Emily Gregory - UNICORNS, DRAGONS, WASP

Niklaas Green - WOMEN

Greta - STAR

President Guedder - STAR

Ham - WATERS

Ferris Hamilton - COAL

Maggy Hamilton - AUSTINS, MOON, ANTI-MUFFINS

Harry [one of the twins] - SUN

Angelique Hawkins - STAR

Dr. Dick Hawkins - STAR

Omni Heno - HOUSE

Ursula Heschel - HOUSE

Norma Hightree - WOMEN

Higgaion [a mammoth] - WATERS

Lucas von Hilpert - WASP

[Max] Maximilliana Sebastiane Horne - HOUSE, TIME

Philip Hunter - YOUNG

[Flip] Philippa Hunter - YOUNG,* WASP

Hal Huxley - AUSTINS

Sister Isobel - WASP

IT [a naked brain] - WRINKLE

Eunice Jackman - YOUNG

Clive James - SUN

Honoria James - SUN

James Therron James - SUN

Terrance Ronald James - SUN

[Ron] Theron James - SUN

Japheth - WATERS

Father Mervin Jason - WASP

Sister Joaquina - LETTERS

Mr. Jenkins - WRINKLE, WIND

Bishop Juxon - WASP

---

* = *protagonist*   ( ) = *maiden name*   SEE TITLE ABBREVIATION CHART PG 179

Karralys - TIME
Klep - TIME
Grandfather Lamech - WATERS
Louise the Larger [a snake] -
    WRINKLE, TIME
Georges Laurens - YOUNG
Paul Laurens - YOUNG
Lucy Leeds -STAR
Rusty Leeds - STAR
Bran Maddox - PLANET
[Beezie] Branwen Zillah Maddox
    O'Keefe - WRINKLE,
    PLANET
[Chuck] Charles Maddox - PLANET
Matthew Maddox - PLANET
Mahlah - WATERS
Jorge Maldonado - STAR
Lt. Esteban Manuel - STAR
Norine Fong Mar - HOUSE
Matred - WATERS
Methuselah - WATERS
Pinky Morrison - COAL
Dean Morton - WASP
Dr. Alex Murry - WRINKLE,
    PLANET, WATERS, TIME
Charles Wallace Murry - WRINKLE,
    WIND, PLANET, WATERS
Dennys Murry - WRINKLE, WIND,
    PLANET, HOUSE,
    WATERS*
Mrs. Kate Murry - WRINKLE,
    WIND, PLANET, WATERS,
    TIME
Lucy Murry - HOUSE
Meg Murry (O'Keefe) - WRINKLE,*
    ARM, WIND,* DRAGONS,
    PLANET,* HOUSE,
    WATERS, TIME
Rhea Murry - HOUSE
Sandy Murry - WRINKLE, WIND,
    PLANET, HOUSE,
    WATERS*

Charlotte Napier - LETTERS*
Patrick Napier - LETTERS
Dame Violet Napier - LETTERS
Captain Nausinio - STAR
Jack Nessinger - STAR
Nan Neville - COAL
Erlund Nikulaussen - WASP
Jacque Nissen - CAMILLA
Bashemath Odega - HOUSE
Oholibamah - WATERS
Leif Olaffsen - WASP
Eric Olaffsen - WASP
Dr. Calvin O'Keefe - WRINKLE,
    WIND, PLANET, ARM,
    DRAGONS, UNICORNS,
    HOUSE,TIME
Charles O'Keefe - ARM,
    DRAGONS, HOUSE
Dennys O'Keefe - ARM,
    DRAGONS, HOUSE
Johnny O'Keefe - ARM, HOUSE
Paddy O'Keefe - PLANET
Peggy O'Keefe - ARM, HOUSE
Polly O'Keefe - ARM, DRAGONS,
    HOUSE,* TIME*
Rosy O'Keefe - ARM, HOUSE
[Xan] Sandy O'Keefe - ARM,
    DRAGONS, HOUSE
Eric Olaffsen - WASP
Edward Osler - COAL
Owain - STAR
Llewellyn Owens - WASP
Papageno - STAR
Madame Colette Percival - YOUNG
Anna Silverton Porcher - ILSA
Henry Randolf Porcher - ILSA*
Proginoskes [a cherubim] - WIND
Mimi Renier Oppenheimer - LOVE,
    WASP
Edward Osler - COAL
Peregrina - LETTERS
Cousin Forsyth Phair - DRAGONS

---

* = *protagonist*   ( ) = *maiden name*   SEE TITLE ABBREVIATION CHART PG 179

Aunt Leonis Phair - DRAGONS
Quenten Phair - DRAGONS
Prime Coordinator - WRINKLE
Grandmother Renier - WASP
Uncle Hoadley Renier - SUN
Aunt Irene Renier - SUN
[Mado] Marguerite Dominique de la
    Valeuv Renier - SUN
Margaret Renier - SUN
Great Aunt Mary Desborough Renier
    - SUN
Great Aunt Olivia Renier - SUN,
    COAL
[Renny] Queron Renier - HOUSE,
Simon Bolivar Quenton Renier -
    DRAGONS*
Stella Renier - SUN*
Theron Renier I - SUN
[Therro] Theron Renier II - SUN
[Terry] Theron Renier III - SUN
Commander Rodney - AUSTINS,
    MOON, RING
Jacky Rodney - RING
Leo Rodney - RING
Nancy Rodney - RING
Bill Rowan - CAMILLA
Frank Rowen - CAMILLA, HOUSE,
    COAL
Dr. Louisa Rowen - CAMILLA,
    COAL
Mona Rowan - CAMILLA
Noel Bouton Saint-Leger - LETTERS
Selah - [a mammoth] - WATERS
Serafino - LETTERS
Manya Sergeievna - RAIN, WASP
Shem - WATERS
Mother Catherine of Siena - WASP
Sporos [a farandola] - WIND
Benji Stone - STAR
[Wolfi] Cardinal Wolfgang von
    Stromberg - WASP

Canon Tom Tallis - ARM,
    UNICORNS, DRAGONS,
    TIME, WOMEN
Tav - TIME
Mr. Theotocopoulous - UNICORNS,
    DRAGONS
Miss Tulip - YOUNG
Tiglah - WATERS
Tynak - TIME
Ugiel [a nephilim] - WATERS
Canon Ulgrade - WASP
Bishop Alwood Undercroft - WASP
Yolanda Xabo Undercroft - WASP
Julie Vigneras - WASP
Justin Michel Vigneras - RAIN,
    WASP
Kristen Vigneras - WASP
Michou Vigneras - WASP
Mrs Whatsit - WRINKLE
Abby Wheaton - WOMEN
Adair Wheaton - WOMEN
Alice Wheaton - WOMEN
Bahama Wheaton - WOMEN
Billy Wheaton - WOMEN
Chantal Wheaton - WOMEN
David Wheaton - WOMEN
Edith Wheaton - WOMEN
Elizabeth Wheaton - WOMEN
Emma Wheaton - WOMEN*
Etienne Wheaton - WOMEN
Everard Wheaton - WOMEN
Harriet Wheaton - WOMEN
Inez Wheaton - WOMEN
Jarvis Wheaton - WOMEN
Louis Wheaton - WOMEN
Marical Wheaton - WOMEN
Meredith Wheaton - WOMEN
Myrlo Wheaton - WOMEN
Sophie Wheaton - WOMEN
Mrs Which - WRINKLE
Mrs Who - WRINKLE

---

* = *protagonist*   ( ) = *maiden name*   SEE TITLE ABBREVIATION CHART PG 179

Elizabeth Wickoff - COAL
James Ansley Wickoff - COAL
Willy [one of the twins] - SUN
[Art] Artaxias Xanthakos - COAL
    [Frankie] Frances Xanthakos -
    COAL
[Mac] Macarios Xanthakos - COAL
Olivia Xanthakos - COAL
Raffi Xanthakos - COAL
[Taxi] Artaxias Xanthakos - COAL
Thessaly Xanthakos - COAL
[Milly] Milcah Adah Zenda -
    HOUSE
Yalith - WATERS
Jean Paul Yvert - WASP
Miss Zeloski - HOUSE
Belle Zenumin - SUN
Jimmy Zenumin - SUN
Prince Otto Zlatovitec - STAR
El Zorco - STAR

NOTE FROM THE AUTHOR: All of the major and most important minor characters of Madeleine's fiction have been listed here. The list also includes a select few of Madeleine's special non-human characters. I take full responsibility for any errors of omission with regard to either characters or book assignments. I have sought to identify briefly certain characters which might be somewhat obscure. I have not included the short play, *18 Washington Square,* or two short fantasies, *Dance in the Desert* and *The Sphinx at Dawn,* in this tabulation.

---

* = *protagonist*   ( ) = *maiden name*   SEE TITLE ABBREVIATION CHART PG 179

APPENDIX G
Madeleine L'Engle on the Web

More and more individuals are turning to the web for information about everyone and everything they are interested in. This is true of those looking for information about Madeleine L'Engle. Individuals interested in finding L'Engle sources and information on the web may simply type in her name at the appropriate space using their favorite search engine to find multiple responses. Many of these responses are simply advertisements of Madeleine's books or sparse pages only infrequently updated. However, I have identified three URL addresses, as of the preparation of the Second Edition, that are rich in content, well-organized, and updated regularly:

The Tesseract: A Madeleine L'Engle Bibliography
in 5 Dimensions
designed by Karen Funk Blocher.
http://members.aol.com/kfbofpql/LEngl.html

Karen has described her page as follows: "The Tesseract is an online bibliography and L'Engle reader's resource, with a brief bio, moderately in-depth book listings and a frequently asked questions section. Judging from the responses, the site seems to provide a major resource for children's book reports as well as answering general questions from both children and adults."

The Madeleine L'Engle WWW Resource
by Chris Smith.
http://www.bonastra.home.ml.org/

Chris says this about his site: "Among the resources available on the main page are Madeleine's speaking schedule for the current year, addresses where one can send a postal letter to Madeleine, search engines which will allow the user to search the Web's largest used book sales databases for L'Engle books. The remainder of the site is subdivided into seven sections: resources for the casual or serious L'Engle fan, interviews with/articles about Madeleine, summaries and reviews of Madeleine's works, the e-mail discussion community, the Bonastra bookstore, a chatroom for L'Engle fans, and a guest book."

The Wheaton College, Buswell Library Special Collections Web Site
http://www.wheaton.edu/learnres/arcsc/collects/sc03/
contain/htm.

Madeleine's papers are archived in the Special Collections of Buswell Library at Wheaton College in Wheaton, Illinois. The collection is extensive. This web page is divided into four main parts: About the Author, About the Collection, Collection Inventory, and Related Materials. The section titled "Collection Inventory" lists page after page of Madeleine's collected papers. The list includes biographical material, photographs, correspondence, manuscripts, poems, articles and reviews by Madeleine, and sermons and addresses. These items are not displayed, only listed. Some of these materials are accessible by researchers; however, special written permission from Madeleine is required for access to much of the collection.

NOTES

NOTES

Foreword
1. From the poem "The Windows" by George Herbert.

Introduction
1. *Walking on Water*, p. 55.
2. Letter to Madeleine L'Engle from Carole Chase, January 11, 1984.
3. Some of the L'Engle Collection at the Wheaton College Library is open to the public. Other materials require special permission from Madeleine.

Chapter I: Madeleine, the Storyteller
1. *A Circle of Quiet*, p. 120.
2. *The Small Rain*, p. ix.
3. *Camilla Dickinson* was first published by Simon & Schuster in 1951, reissued as *Camilla* in 1965 by Delacorte Press and in 1982 by Dell Publishing Co., Inc.
4. Canon Tallis appears in *Dragons in the Waters, The Arm of the Starfish, The Young Unicorns*, and *Certain Women*.
5. "Lines after Sir Thomas Browne," *The Weather of the Heart*, p. 20.
6. In *The Arm of the Starfish* and *Dragons in the Waters*, we meet Poly O'Keefe. This young protagonist becomes "Polly" O'Keefe in *A House Like a Lotus*.
7. *Walking on Water*, p. 25.
8. *Walking on Water*, p. 161.
9. *Walking on Water*, p. 161.
10. *Walking on Water*, p. 149.
11. *Walking on Water*, p. 149.
12. *Walking on Water*, p. 149.
13. *Walking on Water*, p. 149.
14. *Walking on Water*, p. 179.
15. *Walking on Water*, p. 162.
16. *Walking on Water*, p. 195.
17. *Walking on Water*, p. 194.
18. *Walking on Water*, p. 137.
19. *Walking on Water*, p. 106.

20. *Walking on Water*, p. 109.
21. This quotation is taken from the speech that Calvin L. Porter made upon presenting Madeleine L'Engle with a Doctor of Humane Letters degree on May 23, 1982.
22. *Encyclopaedia Britannica*, 15th ed., *Micropaedia*, vol. 8, p. 220, 1974.

Chapter II: The Master Storybook

1. *The Rock That Is Higher*, p. 93.
2. These statements are taken from a personal letter to me in which Madeleine answered some of my questions about her use of and relationship to the Bible.
3. Ibid.
4. Ibid.
5. *The Irrational Season*, p. 100.
6. *The Irrational Season*, p. 100.
7. *A Wrinkle in Time*, pp. 67-68.
8. *A Wrinkle in Time*, pp. 201-2.
9. *A Ring of Endless Light*, p. 44.
10. *A Ring of Endless Light*, p. 44.
11. This description is part of a comment by *The Washington Post Book World* that appeared on the back cover of the Sunburst edition of *The Journey with Jonah* published in 1991 by Farrar, Straus & Giroux.
12. *Dance in the Desert*, p. 1.
13. *The Irrational Season*, pp. 125-26.
14. *And It Was Good*, p. 79.
15. *The Irrational Season*, p. 114.
16. *The Rock That Is Higher*, p. 89.
17. See particularly the discussion in *The Rock That Is Higher*, Chapter 4, "Story as the Search for Truth," pp. 89-99.
18. *Sold into Egypt*, p. 16.
19. *Sold into Egypt*, p. 164.
20. *The Rock That Is Higher*, p. 215.
21. *A Stone for a Pillow*, p. 80.
22. *A Stone for a Pillow*, p. 81.
23. *The Rock That Is Higher*, pp. 214-15.
24. *A Stone for a Pillow*, p. 66.
25. *The Rock That Is Higher*, p. 180.
26. *Bright Evening Star*, p. 144.
27. *Penguins and Golden Calves*, p. 134.
28. *Penguins and Golden Calves*, p. 118.

Chapter III: The Creator of Galaxies

1. *A Stone for a Pillow*, pp. 123-24.
2. *Walking on Water*, p. 118.
3. Members of the clergy appear in several works of fiction by Madeleine L'Engle, including: *Meet the Austins*, *The Arm of the Starfish*, *The Love Letters*, *The Other Side of the Sun*, *Dragons in the Waters*, *A Ring of Endless Light*, *A Severed Wasp*, *An Acceptable Time*, and *Certain Women*.
4. *Meet the Austins*, p. 183.
5. *Meet the Austins*, p. 161.
6. *Meet the Austins*, p. 153. These words of Hildevert of Lavardin, who lived about 1125 A.D., are one of Grandfather's favorite sayings.
7. *A Stone for a Pillow*, p. 86.
8. See also *The Rock That Is Higher*, p. 83.
9. *The Moon by Night*, pp. 132-37.
10. *The Moon by Night*, p. 142.
11. *The Moon by Night*, p. 142.
12. See *The Summer of the Great-grandmother*, pp. 64, 71-72, and *Two-Part Invention*, pp. 108, 123-25.
13. See also *Sold into Egypt*, p. 61.
14. *The Moon by Night*, p. 145.
15. *The Moon by Night*, p. 208.
16. *The Moon by Night*, p. 208.
17. *Sold into Egypt*, p. 136.
18. *A Ring of Endless Light*, p. 64.
19. *A Ring of Endless Light*, p. 8.
20. *A Ring of Endless Light*, p. 19.
21. *A Stone for a Pillow*, p. 87.
22. *A Ring of Endless Light*, p. 290.
23. *A Wrinkle in Time*'s Meg Murry grew up and married Calvin O'Keefe. Polly is one of the O'Keefes' seven children.
24. Bishop Colubra is the third of Madeleine's characters based on a real person. He is based on David Somerville, retired archbishop of Vancouver.
25. *An Acceptable Time*, p. 45-46.
26. *The Rock That Is Higher*, p. 122.
27. *Penguins and Golden Calves*, p. 94.
28. *An Acceptable Time*, p. 237.
29. In *The Rock That Is Higher*, pp. 218-19, Madeleine hints at a possible beginning step in understanding the mystery, when she discusses the modern physics discovery that energy and matter are interchangeable. Perhaps, she suggests, the energy that was the Christ transformed itself into the physical matter that we know as the man Jesus.
30. *A Stone for a Pillow*, p. 86.
31. *The Rock That Is Higher*, p. 218.

32. *Sold into Egypt*, p. 20
33. *An Acceptable Time*, p. 314.
34. *Sold into Egypt*, p. 28.
35. *And It Was Good*, p. 81.
36. *And It Was Good*, p. 163.
37. *An Acceptable Time*, p. 291.
38. *An Acceptable Time*, pp. 330-31. Bishop Langland lived about 1400 A.D.
39. *Bright Evening Star*, p. 32.
40. *And It Was Good*, p. 46.
41. *A Stone for a Pillow*, p. 140.
42. *Sold into Egypt*, p. 59.
43. *Bright Evening Star*, p. 32.
44. *Bright Evening Star*, p. 33.
45. Personal statement made in conversation.

Chapter IV: Light-Bearers

1. *Sold into Egypt*, p. 20.
2. *Penguins and Golden Calves*, p. 63.
3. *Penguins and Golden Calves*, p. 69.
4. *Sold into Egypt*, p. 97.
5. *Bright Evening Star*, p. 80.
6. *Bright Evening Star*, p. 86.
7. *Bright Evening Star*, p. 78.
8. *And It Was Good*, p. 67.
9. In *The Moon by Night*, p. 134.
10. *A Ring of Endless Light*, p. 20.
11. *A Ring of Endless Light*, p. 20.
12. *The Summer of the Great-grandmother*, p. 49.
13. *A Wrinkle in Time*, pp. 207-208.
14. *The Weather of the Heart*, p. 16.
15. *A Wrinkle in Time*, pp. 193-95.
16. *The Rock That Is Higher*, p. 205.
17. *An Acceptable Time*, pp. 330-31.
18. *A Ring of Endless Light*, p. 75.
19. *Sold into Egypt*, p. 200.
20. *A Wrinkle in Time*, pp. 158-59.
21. *The Rock That Is Higher*, p. 88.
22. *The Irrational Season*, p. 112.
23. *Sold into Egypt*, p. 20.
24. *And It Was Good*, p. 55.
25. *And It Was Good*, p. 55.

26. *The Rock That Is Higher*, pp. 46-47.
27. *Sold into Egypt*, p. 24.
28. *A Wrinkle in Time*, p. 160.
29. *A Wrinkle in Time*, p. 160.
30. *And Both Were Young*, pp. 16-17.
31. *A Wind in the Door*, p. 78.
32. *Sold into Egypt*, p. 101; see also p. 92.
33. *Sold into Egypt*, p. 69.
34. *Sold into Egypt*, p. 159.
35. *A Ring of Endless Light*, p. 164.
36. *Sold into Egypt*, p. 191.
37. *Sold into Egypt*, p. 15.
38. *A Wind in the Door*, p. 178.
39. *A Wind in the Door*, p. 190.

Chapter V: The Family Table

1. *A Ring of Endless Light*, pp. 78-79.
2. *The Rock That Is Higher*, p. 44.
3. A fourth family, the O'Keefes, should also be noted. Mrs. O'Keefe is Meg Murry grown up and married to Calvin O'Keefe, a biologist doing research on starfish arm regeneration. The O'Keefes have seven children, of whom Polly O'Keefe, their oldest daughter, is the protagonist in *A House Like a Lotus* and *An Acceptable Time*.
4. The O'Keefes are also a two-parent family. Meg O'Keefe is a computer and mathematics whiz who helps her husband with his research on starfish regeneration.
5. *A Circle of Quiet*, p. 220.
6. Madeleine's purely fictional families live out their lives in chronological time (*chronos*), while her fantasy families operate in nonlinear time (*kairos*). Several of her fictional characters have met, interacted with, and even married characters from her fantasies. See Appendix E (page 179) for diagrams of some of the relationships among these characters.
7. *The Rock That Is Higher*, p. 48.
8. *A Wrinkle in Time*, p. 210.
9. Vicky Austin also appears later in *Troubling a Star*, a story about her adventuresome trip to Antarctica.
10. *A Ring of Endless Light*, pp. 82-83.
11. *Meet the Austins*, p. 124.
12. *Meet the Austins*, p. 11.
13. *The Summer of the Great-grandmother*, p. 233.
14. *The Summer of the Great-grandmother*, p. 233.

15. *Certain Women*, p. 3.
16. *Meet the Austins*, pp. 38-41.
17. *Meet the Austins*, p. 40.
18. *Meet the Austins*, pp. 40-41.
19. *Meet the Austins*, p. 41.
20. *Meet the Austins*, pp. 66-69.
21. *Meet the Austins*, pp. 102-105.
22. *A Ring of Endless Light*, pp. 74-76.
23. *The Moon by Night*, p. 134.
24. *The Moon by Night*, p. 75.
25. *The Summer of the Great-grandmother*, pp. 84-85.
26. *Sold into Egypt*, p. 131.
27. *The Rock That Is Higher*, p. 56.
28. *A Ring of Endless Light*, p. 79.
29. *The Irrational Season*, p. 212.
30. *The Irrational Season*, pp. 211-12.
31. *Two-Part Invention*, p. 181.
32. *A Live Coal in the Sea*, p. 92.
33. *A Live Coal in the Sea*, p. 101.
34. *A Live Coal in the Sea*, p. 105.
35. *Penguins and Golden Calves*, pp. 45-46.
36. *Penguins and Golden Calves*, pp. 14, 15, 50.
37. *Mothers and Daughters*, p. 19.
38. *Friends for the Journey*, p. 9.
39. *Friends for the Journey*, p. 134.
40. *Bright Evening Star*, p. 137.
41. *Bright Evening Star*, p. 137.
42. *Bright Evening Star*, p. 138.
43. Madeleine receives far more letters from grown-ups and she answers them, too.
44. *A Circle of Quiet*, p. 106.
45. *A Circle of Quiet*, p. 99.

Chapter VI: Sacred Community

1. *A Stone for a Pillow*, p. 18.
2. *The Irrational Season*, pp. 64-65.
3. *The Irrational Season*, p. 67.
4. *The Irrational Season*, p. 68.
5. *And It Was Good*, p. 145.
6. *Two-Part Invention*, p. 39.
7. *The Rock That Is Higher*, p. 159.
8. *The Rock That Is Higher*, p. 159.

9. *The Rock That Is Higher*, p. 159.
10. *And It Was Good*, p. 146.
11. *The Irrational Season*, p. 17.
12. This poem was part of the Christmas letter Madeleine sent in 1992.
13. *The Irrational Season*, pp. 87-88.
14. *The Irrational Season*, pp. 90-91.
15. *The Rock That Is Higher*, pp. 173-74.
16. *The Irrational Season*, pp. 158-59.
17. Madeleine also has a familial connection with ministers in the person of her son-in-law, Alan Jones, who is an Episcopal priest and the author of several books on spirituality.
18. *A Severed Wasp*, p. 82.
19. *A Severed Wasp*, p. 60
20. *A Severed Wasp*, p. 60.
21. *Friends for the Journey*, p. 172.
22. *Sold into Egypt*, p. 157.
23. Madeleine asked me this question during a telephone conversation.
24. *The Irrational Season*, p. 141.
25. *Bright Evening Star*, pp. 100-101.
26. *A Stone for a Pillow*, pp. 165-66.
27. *Bright Evening Star*, pp. 94-95.
28. *The Rock That Is Higher*, p. 103.
29. Madeleine told me this in answer to my question during a phone conversation.
30. *Two-Part Invention*, p. 207.
31. *The Irrational Season*, p. 94.
32. *A Stone for a Pillow*, p. 77.

Chapter VII: The Butterfly Effect

1. *The Irrational Season*, p. 214.
2. *The Rock That Is Higher*, p. 225.
3. *The Rock That Is Higher*, p. 223.
4. *A Stone for a Pillow*, p. 42.
5. *Troubling a Star*, p. 146.
6. *A Live Coal in the Sea*, p. 172.
7. *A Stone for a Pillow*, p. 97.
8. *A Circle of Quiet*, p. 97.
9. *Sold into Egypt*, p. 70.
10. *Sold into Egypt*, p. 70.
11. *Sold into Egypt*, p. 167.
12. *A Wind in the Door*, p. 183.

13. *A Ring of Endless Light*, pp. 12-13.
14. *A Ring of Endless Light*, p. 24.
15. *A Ring of Endless Light*, p. 166.
16. *Sold into Egypt*, p. 70.
17. *The Irrational Season*, p. 58.
18. *A Ring of Endless Light*, p. 44.
19. *A Ring of Endless Light*, p. 44.
20. *A Ring of Endless Light*, p. 207.
21. *A Ring of Endless Light*, p. 207.
22. *Two-Part Invention*, pp. 171-72.
23. *Certain Women*, p. 189.
24. *Certain Women*, p. 18.
25. *Sold into Egypt*, pp. 99-100.
26. *Bright Evening Star*, pp. 113-114.
27. *Bright Evening Star*, pp. 115-116.
28. *Camilla*, p. 199.
29. *Camilla*, p. 199.
30. *A Severed Wasp*, p. 160.
31. *A Severed Wasp*, p. 161.
32. *A Severed Wasp*, p. 161.
33. *A Severed Wasp*, p. 161.
34. *The Rock That Is Higher*, p. 67.
35. *A Stone for a Pillow*, p. 98.
36. *The Rock That Is Higher*, p. 51.
37. *A Stone for a Pillow*, pp. 99-102.
38. *A Stone for a Pillow*, p. 99.
39. *Sold into Egypt*, p. 99.
40. *The Summer of the Great-grandmother*, pp. 187-88.
41. *The Other Side of the Sun*, pp. 18 and 31.
42. *Sold into Egypt*, p. 59.
43. *A Live Coal in the Sea*, p. 167.
44. *The Rock That Is Higher*, p. 243.
45. *The Rock That Is Higher*, p. 243.
46. *The Rock That Is Higher*, p. 245.
47. *A Stone for a Pillow*, p. 84.
48. *A Stone for a Pillow*, p. 84.
49. "Dialogue: Madeleine L'Engle on Religion and Literature," *National Catholic Register*, August 18, 1985, p. 6.

Chapter VIII: Beyond Gender Myths

1. *And It Was Good*, p. 18.

2. This quotation is taken from a personal letter to me from Madeleine, dated January 26, 1984.
3. *Sold into Egypt*, p. 19.
4. "Shake the Universe," *Ms.*, July/August 1987, p. 182.
5. *Dragons in the Waters, The Arm of the Starfish,* and *Many Waters* are three of Madeleine's books that have male protagonists.
6. *Many Waters*, p. 198.
7. *The Irrational Season*, p. 8.
8. *Walking on Water*, p. 90.
9. *Walking on Water*, p. 90.
10. *A Severed Wasp*, p. 238.
11. "Shake the Universe," p. 182.
12. "Shake the Universe," p. 182.
13. *And It Was Good*, p. 18.
14. *And It Was Good*, p. 18.
15. *The Rock That Is Higher*, p. 136.
16. *The Rock That Is Higher*, pp. 135-36.
17. *The Rock That Is Higher*, p. 136.
18. *A Stone for a Pillow*, p. 144.
19. *The Rock That Is Higher*, p. 27.
20. *The Rock That Is Higher*, p. 45.
21. *Sold into Egypt*, p. 73.
22. *Sold into Egypt*, p. 76.
23. *The Rock That Is Higher*, p. 122.
24. *And It Was Good*, pp. 17-18.
25. *And It Was Good*, p. 25.
26. *A Ring of Endless Light*, p. 76.
27. *The Irrational Season*, p. 7.
28. *An Acceptable Time*, p. 98.
29. *A Stone for a Pillow*, p. 110.
30. *Bright Evening Star*, pp. 93-94.
31. *Bright Evening Star*, p. 94.
32. *Bright Evening Star*, p. 94.
33. *Bright Evening Star*, p. 94.
34. *Bright Evening Star*, p. 94.

Chapter IX: Madeleine, the Mystic

1. *The Rock That Is Higher*, p. 266.
2. *Walking on Water*, p. 149.
3. *And It Was Good*, p. 136.
4. *And It Was Good*, p. 142.

5. From marginal notes Madeleine made on a revised manuscript of this book.
6. *And It Was Good*, p. 140.
7. *Walking on Water*, p. 194.
8. *Walking on Water*, p. 149.
9. *Walking on Water*, p. 185.
10. *The Irrational Season*, p. 120.
11. *The Irrational Season*, p. 120.
12. *The Irrational Season*, pp. 122-23.
13. *The Weather of the Heart*, p. 80.
14. *Bright Evening Star*, p. 25.
15. *Bright Evening Star*, pp. 25-26.
16. *Bright Evening Star*, p. 25.
17. *The Summer of the Great-grandmother*, p. 151.
18. *The Summer of the Great-grandmother*, p. 151.
19. Harkness, Georgia, *Mysticism: Its Meaning and Message* (New York: Abingdon Press, 1973), p. 24.
20. *The Irrational Season*, p. 214-15.
21. *A Stone for a Pillow*, p. 77.
22. *And It Was Good*, pp. 140-41.
23. Harkness, *Mysticism: Its Meaning and Message*, pp. 24-28.
24. *A Wind in the Door*, p. 78.
25. *A Wind in the Door*, p. 99.
26. "Shake the Universe," *Ms.*, July/August 1987, p. 182.
27. Parker Palmer, *The Active Life: Wisdom for Work, Creativity, and Caring* (San Francisco: Harper San Francisco, 1990), p. 8.
28. *The Rock That Is Higher*, p. 197.
29. John R. Yungblut, *Discovering God Within* (Philadelphia: Westminster Press, 1979), p. 45.
30. Palmer, *The Active Life*, p. 8.
31. *Walking on Water*, p. 132.
32. Harkness, *Mysticism: Its Meaning and Message*, p. 24.
33. Madeleine told me this definition personally.
34. *The Rock That Is Higher*, pp. 102-103.
35. *Walking on Water*, p. 179.
36. *Penguins and Golden Calves*, p. 135.

Permission Acknowledgments

Grateful acknowledgment is made for permission to reprint the following copyrighted material:

Quotation from an interview with Madeleine L'Engle in "Dialogue" by John Andriote, *National Catholic Register*, August 18, 1985. Reprinted by permission of National Catholic Register.

Quotation from "prism" in *Encyclopædia Britannica*, 15th edition (1974), VIII:220. Reprinted by permission of Encyclopædia Britannica, Inc.

Quotation from *Mysticism: Its Meaning and Message* by Georgia Harkness. Copyright ©1973 by Abingdon Press. Reprinted by permission of Abingdon Press.

Excerpts from *An Acceptable Time* by Madeleine L'Engle. Copyright © 1989 by Crosswicks, Ltd. Reprinted by permission of Farrar, Straus & Giroux, Inc.

Excerpts from *And It Was Good: Reflections on Beginnings* by Madeleine L'Engle, Copyright © 1983 by Crosswicks, Ltd. Used by permission of Harold Shaw Publishers, Wheaton, IL.

Excerpts from *Bright Evening Star* by Madeleine L'Engle. Copyright © 1997 by Crosswicks, Ltd. Used by permission of Harold Shaw Publishers, Wheaton, IL.

Excerpt from *Camilla* by Madeleine L'Engle. Copyright © 1965 by Crosswicks, Ltd. Reprinted by permission of Dell, a division of Bantam, Doubleday, Dell Publishing Group, Inc.

Excerpts from *Certain Women* by Madeleine L'Engle. Copyright © 1992 by Crosswicks, Ltd. Reprinted by permission of Farrar, Straus & Giroux, Inc.

Excerpts from *A Circle of Quiet* by Madeleine L'Engle. Copyright © 1972 by Madeleine L'Engle Franklin. Reprinted by permission of Farrar, Straus & Giroux, Inc.

Excerpt from *Dance in the Desert* by Madeleine L'Engle. Text copyright © 1969 by Madeleine L'Engle Franklin. Reprinted by permission of Farrar, Straus & Giroux, Inc.

Excerpts from *Friends for the Journey* by Luci Shaw and Madeleine L'Engle. Copyright © 1997 by Luci Shaw and Madeleine L'Engle . Reprinted by permission of Servant Publications, Box 8617, Ann Arbor, MI 48107.

Excerpts from *The Irrational Season* by Madeleine L'Engle. Copyright © 1977 by Crosswicks, Ltd. Reprinted by permission of HarperCollins Publishers.

Excerpts from *A Live Coal in the Sea* by Madeleine L'Engle. Copyright © 1996 by Crosswicks, Ltd. Published by Farrar, Straus & Giroux, Inc.

INDEX

INDEX*

- A -

Acceptable Time, An, 31, 38 63,
     64q, 65q, 66, 67q, 77, 80,
     139, 142, 147q
All Angels Episcopal Church, 117,
     119
Anaral, 67, 85, 139, 147
And Both Were Young, 32, 82
*And It Was Good: Reflections on
     Beginnings,* 36, 37, 52q, 64,
     75, 80q, 110q, 137q, 143q,
     146q, 152q, 157q
Andriote, John, 135
Anglican boarding school, 31, 45,
     81, 108, 109
     See also L'Engle, Madeleine,
     education of
Antarctica, 39, 122, 196n9
Anytime Prayers, 39
Aqueduct Conference Center, 29,
     30, 37, 116
Archer, Joshua, 153
Arm of the Starfish, The, 34, 153,
     200n5
artists, 41, 42, 63, 135, 157, 158,
     159
     See also creativity
Ascension Episcopal Church, 108
Ashley Hall, 31, 46, 108, 109
     See also L'Engle, Madeleine,
     education of
astrophysics, 50, 63, 121, 122, 158,
     194n29
Aunt Beast, 47
Aunt Elena, *See* **Huxley, Elena**

Austin family, 32, 33, 34, 36, 48,
     59, 60, 62, 64, 75, 79, 83, 88,
     90-95, 97, 98, 99, 122, 125,
     142, 143, 146, 181
Austin, Douglas, 60, 61, 90, 94, 95
Austin, John, 59, 87, 90, 91, 92,
     93, 94, 97
Austin, Rob, 32, 90, 93
Austin, Suzy, 90, 91, 93, 94, 95,
     98, 125, 142, 146, 147
     See also **Davidson, Dr. Suzy**
Austin, Vicky, 48, 49, 59,
     60-63, 64, 75, 77, 83, 90, 91,
     92, 93, 95, 97, 122, 125-27,
     142, 196n9
Austin, Mrs. (Victoria Eaton),
     36, 88, 90, 91, 92-93, 94, 146
Austin, Dr. Wallace, 90, 91, 93,
     142-43
     See also **Eaton, Grandfather**
awards and honors, 33, 43, 170-73,
     193nl21

-B-

Bible
     in L'Engle's fiction, 47, 48, 75
     in L'Engle's nonfiction, 36, 49,
     51-56, 144-46
     L'Engle's interpretation of, 46,
     52-55, 66, 144, 145, 147
     L'Engle's reading of, 18, 36, 43,
     45-47, 55, 58, 152, 193n2
     quotations from, 47, 48, 55, 75,
     147
     See also biblical characters;
     biblical stories; Psalms

---

* *Book titles are shown in italics, fictional characters in bold face, q=quotation , n=note.*

biblical characters
  Asenath, 145
  Bildah, 145
  Daniel, 54
  King David, 39, 100
  Deborah, 145
  Dinah, 145
  Esther, 145
  Ezekiel, 54
  Isaiah, 118
  Jacob, 57, 84, 138, 144
  Jael, 145
  Jonah, 34, 49, 54
  Joseph, 37, 84, 85, 145
  Mary Magdalene, 149
  Moses, 40
  Paul, 73
  Rachel, 144
  Shechem, 145
  See also biblical stories; Jesus the
    Christ
biblical stories, 18, 36, 37, 39, 40,
  45, 49, 50-51, 52-54, 56, 80,
  84-85, 144-45
Bodeway, Bishop Felix, 36, 48, 79,
  98, 112, 113, 115, 133, 142
Book of Common Prayer, The, 46,
  115
Bowman, Wesley, 48
Bright Evening Star, 40, 52, 56q, 68,
  69q, 74q, 102q, 118q, 128,
  148, 149q, 155q
Brown, Thomas, 75
Buswell Memorial Library,
  See Wheaton College
butterfly effect, 63, 121-23, 158

-C-
calendar, Christian, See church,
  year
Camazotz, 47, 77, 78, 81

Camilla, 128, 129q, 192n13
Camilla Dickinson, 32, 39, 192n13
Camp, Charles, 30, 31, 87, 96, 109,
  119, 128
Camp, Madeleine, 30, 35, 76, 87,
  91, 96, 132
Cathedral of St. John the Divine,
  19, 26, 33, 34, 36, 38, 46, 48,
  98, 107-108, 110, 111, 112,
  113, 117, 119, 135
  in L'Engle's fiction, 36, 48, 98,
    112, 113, 114, 115, 119
Certain Women, 38, 39, 48, 92q,
  100, 127q
Chase, Carole, 13-15, 17-18, 21-22,
  25-27, 39, 103, 115-16, 151,
  217
Chase, Mary Ellen, 46
children, See L'Engle, Madeleine, as
  children's writer; L'Engle,
  childhood and family of;
  L'Engle, marriage and family of
choice, See freedom of choice
Christ, See Jesus the Christ
Christian Theological Seminary, 43
Christmas, 22, 38, 40, 82, 95, 110
chronos, 196n6
church
  denominations, 66, 109, 116,
    117
  nature of, 92, 114-17, 118, 120
  sacraments of, See Eucharist;
    liturgy
  universal, 116-18
    See also ecumenism
  year, 35, 110, 111
  See also L'Engle, Madeleine,
    relationship with church
Circle of Quiet, A, 29q, 34, 46, 89q,
  103q, 104, 105q, 123q, 140
clergy, See ministers
co-creation, 52, 63, 83, 156, 159

Colubra, Bishop Nason, 38, 64, 65, 67, 77, 79, 142, 194n24
communion, *See* Eucharist
community, 80-81, 107, 109, 114, 117, 118, 119
Congregational Church (Goshen, Conn.), 109, 115, 117, 119
consumerism, 73, 124, 126
cosmos, *See* universe
Creation, 54, 55, 56, 59, 66, 69, 76, 80, 82, 83, 118, 121, 122, 159
creativity, 25, 41-42, 54, 63, 159, 176
   See also artists
Creator, *See* God
Crosswicks, 26, 32, 33, 34, 35, 58, 61, 71-72, 92, 98, 109, 113, 122, 123
Crosswicks Journals, 21, 34, 35, 38
cryonics, 49, 126

- D -
Dance in the Desert, 34, 49, 50q
Davidson family, 88, 98-99, 100, 181
   Davidson, Dean Josiah, 98
   Davidson, Dr. Suzy Austin, 98, 142
death, 29, 31, 38, 48-49, 53, 61, 62, 63, 66, 73, 77, 78, 83-84, 91, 92-93, 99, 108, 111, 119, 125-26, 128, 135
deepening, 76, 84, 124
denominations, *See* church, denominations
Diary of Anne Frank, The, 60, 95
Dickinson family, 39, 78, 115, 148, 183
   Dickinson, Camilla, 39, 67, 78, 100, 101, 115, 123, 148
     See also Xanthakos, Camilla

dinner table, 32, 59, 73, 87, 91, 96-97, 99, 146
divorce, 98, 99, 103, 113
dolphins, 25, 83, 121, 125, 128
Dorcas, *See* Gibson, Dorcas
Dragons in the Waters, 200n5

- E -
Easter, 66, 111
Eaton, Grandfather, 48, 49, 59-60, 61, 62-63, 75, 78, 79, 90, 92, 94, 95, 97, 125, 127, 142
ecumenism, 116-17, 158
Eddington, Adam, 83-84, 87, 97, 122, 125, 153
18 Washington Square, South: A Comedy in One Act, 31, 88
Einstein, Albert, 59, 60
El, 68, 118, 146
   See also God
environment, 123-25, 126, 128, 131, 133, 137, 158
   See also consumerism; interconnectedness; interdependence
Eucharist, 97, 111-12, 116, 117, 119, 154
evil, *See* good

- F -
fact vs. truth, *See* truth
faith, 22, 27, 34, 35, 41, 43, 52, 55, 56, 60-62, 68, 105, 118, 151, 159
fallibility, 78, 114, 156
family
   extended, 98-99, 102-103
   of God, 125, 131, 134, 158
   nature of, 80-81, 87, 88, 90, 91, 95-96, 101-103, 131, 141, 196n6

FAMILY (CONTINUED)
   See also Austin family; Davidson
      family; Dickinson family; Holy
      Family; L'Engle, Madeleine,
      childhood and family of;
      L'Engle, Madeleine, marriage
      and family of; Murry family;
      O'Keefe family; Wheaton
      family; Xanthakos family
female, *See* women
feminism, 14, 25-26, 27, 137-39,
   142, 145, 148
forgiveness, 18, 39, 48, 49, 56, 64,
   67, 75, 78, 79, 80, 100, 103,
   112, 115, 119
Forrester, Katherine, 31, 36, 113
   See also **Vigneras, Katherine**
Franklin, Bion, 32, 33, 71
   See also **Austin, Rob**
Franklin, Hugh, 32, 33, 35, 37-38,
   39, 76, 88, 91, 92, 96, 98,
   108-109, 110, 138, 147
   illness and death of, 38, 39, 73,
      92, 99, 119
Franklin, Josephine, *See* Jones,
   Josephine Franklin
Franklin, Laurie, 71-72
freedom of choice, 21, 61, 69, 74,
   77, 82, 85, 141-44
Friends for the Journey, 40, 102q,
   116q
friendship, 18, 22, 39, 40, 41, 73,
   99, 101-102, 109, 116, 132

- G -

galaxies, *See* stars
gender, 64-65, 137, 140, 142, 146,
   148, 149, 158
Genesis, 36-37, 54, 80, 152
Genesis Trilogy, 36-37, 52, 64
Gibson, Dorcas, 133, 141-42
Glimpses of Grace, 39

Glorious Impossible, The, 38
God
   as Creator, 47, 53-56, 57-59, 63,
      66, 67, 68, 69, 73-75, 80, 82,
      83, 111, 121, 126, 146-47,
      149, 159
   grace of, 20, 35, 39, 49, 56, 67,
      76, 78-79, 84, 97, 100, 102,
      114, 115, 126, 133, 134, 135
   image of, 76, 80, 84, 146-47,
      149, 157
   love of, 56, 63, 65-69, 73, 75, 79,
      81, 83, 98, 108, 114, 126,
      133, 154, 156-58
   as male/female, 64-65, 146-47, 149
   nature of, 18, 20, 35, 37,39, 42,
      48, 49, 52-56, 57-63, 65-69,
      73-80, 81, 83-85, 98, 100,
      110, 111, 113-14, 117-18,
      121, 124, 128, 131, 133, 135,
      144, 146, 151, 152, 153,
      156-58
   of Universe, 42, 56, 66, 81, 111,
      126, 145, 153, 158
   See also L'Engle, Madeleine,
      relationship with God
godchildren, 99, 102
God-stories, 52
   See also biblical stories
good, 21, 84, 85, 93, 94, 135
Gospel, *See* Bible
grace, *See* God, grace of
Gray, Zachary, 48-49, 60, 61, 64,
   65, 66-67, 77-78, 89, 90, 95,
   97, 126, 143
Greatie, 132
grief, 31, 108, 119, 125

- H -

hallowing, 66, 126
Hamilton, Maggy, 32, 90, 92-93,
   94, 143

Hanukkah, 95
Harkness, Georgia, 156, 157, 158q
Hildevert of Lavardin, 59, 194n6
Holy Family, 34, 50, 81
Holy Spirit, 112, 126, 153-54
Holy Week, 111
homosexuality, 100, 133
Honoria, 132-33
House Like a Lotus, A, 37
human body, 73
human nature, 14, 20, 21, 47,
    52-53, 55, 58, 61, 63, 66, 68,
    71, 72-74, 77-85, 101,
    112-16, 124, 127-29, 131,
    133, 135, 140, 143, 144,
    146-47, 149, 156-57
humility, 74, 82, 117, 158
Hunter, Philippa, 82
Huxley, Elena, 92, 94
Huxley, Hal, 91, 92, 93

- I -
icons/idols, 39, 52, 53, 55, 56, 58,
    68, 73, 80, 101
idolatry, 102
Ilsa, 31, 90
image of God, *See* God, image of
images, 52, 58, 68, 77, 159
incarnation, 40, 56, 65-66, 73-74,
    97, 110, 118, 128, 156, 157,
    158, 194n29
injustice, *See* justice
inspiration, 42, 52, 72, 154
interconnectedness, 63, 74, 121-23,
    131, 158
interdependence, 80, 107, 122, 132,
    135
intuition, 42, 44, 53, 58, 104, 142,
    144, 159

Irrational Season, The, 34, 35, 46,
    51-52q, 53q, 79q, 97-98q,
    108q, 110q, 111, 112q, 117q,
    119q, 121q, 140q, 147q, 153-
    154q, 156q
IT, 76, 77, 78, 81, 134

- J -
Jenkins, Mr., 76, 84
Jesus the Christ, 19, 38, 40, 50-51,
    54, 65-66, 71, 73-75, 77, 79,
    81, 102, 110-11, 114, 117,
    128, 134, 135, 149, 152, 153,
    155, 156, 194n29
"Jesus Prayer," 152
jokes, 94
Jones, Alan, 155, 198n17
Jones, Charlotte, 38, 99, 102, 155
Jones, Josephine Franklin, 32, 33,
    110, 155
Jones, Léna, 99, 102, 155
Journey with Jonah, The, 34, 49
justice, 60, 123, 130, 133, 134, 135,
    149
Juxon, Bishop, 114

- K -
kairos, 26, 196n6
Kilby, Clyde, 35
Klep, 66

- L -
labels, 33, 148, 158
Langland, Bishop William, 67,
    195n38
language, inclusive, 64, 147-48

L'Engle, Madeleine
awards, 170-73, 174-78
books by, 163-65, 166-68,
169-73
childhood and family of, 14,
30-31, 45-46, 57, 87-88, 96,
108-109, 128, 138, 146, 155
as children's writer, 33, 39, 49,
103-105, 139, 149
devotional life of, 18, 41-42, 46,
63, 91, 94-95, 102, 115-16,
131, 151-55, 157-58, 160
See also Eucharist
education of, 31, 81, 88,
108-109, 138
importance of books to, 94-95
marriage and family of, 32, 33,
35, 37-40, 73, 76, 80-81,
88-89, 90-92, 94-96, 98, 99,
102, 108-109, 110, 112, 119,
138, 140, 147, 155, 198n17
as mystic, 151-60
poetry by, 21-22, 35, 40, 51-52,
76-77, 97-98, 110-11, 112,
154-55, 160
relationship with church, 46, 58,
92, 108-12, 114-17, 118, 119
relationship with God, 17-21,
27, 30, 33, 36, 54-64, 68-69,
107-109, 116, 146, 152-53,
156, 158-59
as storyteller, 18, 19, 20, 30, 32,
41, 49, 50, 88, 110, 149, 159
See also story
theology of, 18, 27, 33, 47, 52,
58, 67, 110
websites featuring, *See* websites
and writing, 13-14, 17, 22, 25,
27, 31, 32, 33, 41-43, 45, 71,
88, 103, 123, 131, 135, 138,
153-54, 157, 159-60
Lines Scribbled on an Envelope, 21

listening, 25, 42, 64, 65, 67, 107,
152, 153, 159, 160
liturgy, 111, 119, 157
Live Coal in the Sea, A, 39, 67, 78,
100q, 101q, 115, 123q, 133,
148
logos, 65
Lord's Prayer, 152
love
for family, 79-81, 89-91, 93, 98,
100, 103
nature of, 14, 35, 50, 56, 63, 68,
73, 76-77, 80, 82, 115-17,
119-21, 126, 131, 133-34, 156
See also God, love of
Love Letters, The, 33-34

- M -

Mado, 135
male, *See* men
Many Waters, 37, 140q,200n5
Maria, 32, 33, 40
Marion E. Wade Center,
See Wheaton College
marital infidelity, 100, 101, 141
marriage, 100, 109, 140, 141, 142
mealtime, *See* dinner table
Meet the Austins, 32, 59q, 73, 91q,
91q, 93q, 146
men/male, 53, 57, 73, 108, 137-39,
142-44, 146-47, 149, 200n5
mercy, 67, 77-78, 152
metaphor, 17, 45, 51, 53
midrash, 49, 145
ministers, 59, 113, 114, 115, 194n3,
198n17
Mitchell, Maria, 140
Moon by Night, The, 34, 48, 60q,
61q, 64, 75q, 77, 90, 95q
Moses, Prince of Egypt, 40

Mothers and Daughters, 40,
101-102q
motherhood, *See* family
Mr. Jenkins, *See* **Jenkins, Mr.**
Mrs Whatsit, *See* **Whatsit, Mrs**
Mrs Which, *See* **Which, Mrs**
Mrs Who, *See* **Who, Mrs**
Ms. magazine, 139q, 157q
Mundelein College, 116
Murry family, 88, 89-90, 99, 180
   Murry, Charles Wallace, 40,
     47-48, 76, 77, 78, 81, 82, 84,
     89, 90, 124, 134
   Murry, Dennys, 89, 90, 140
   Murry, Meg, 14, 40, 47-48, 76,
     77, 78, 81, 82, 89, 90, 124,
     134, 139, 140, 141, 157,
     194n23
       See also **O'Keefe, Mrs.**
       Meg Murry
   Murry, Mr. (Dr.), 64, 89, 90
   Murry, Mrs. (Dr.), 64, 88, 90,
     139, 148
   Murry, Sandy, 89, 90, 140
mysterium tremendum et fascinans,
   62, 118, 135, 160
mystery, 30, 40, 53, 56, 61, 62, 74,
   111, 116, 154-55
mysticism, 151, 156, 158
   See also L'Engle, Madeleine, as
     mystic
myth, 45, 52, 53, 54, 58, 110, 111

- **N** -

naming, 81, 82, 152, 157, 160
National Catholic Register, 135q
Newbery Medal, 33, 174-78
New York, 13, 26, 30, 31, 32, 33,
     34, 36, 38, 88, 99, 107, 108,
     109, 113, 115, 117, 119, 142

- **O** -

O'Keefe family, 99, 180, 194n23,
   196n3, 196n4
   O'Keefe, Calvin, 47, 89, 90, 76,
     141, 194n23, 196n3
   O'Keefe, Mrs. Meg Murry, 40,
     141, 194n23, 196n3, 196n4
   O'Keefe, Polly, 64, 65, 66-67, 77,
     139, 192n6, 194n23, 196n3
Oppenheimer, Mimi, 98, 114, 142,
   148
Orwell, George, 114
Other Side of the Sun, The, 34,
   132-33
Otto, Rudolf, 62
ousia, 75-76

- **P** -

Palmer, Parker, 157q, 158q
parables, 53, 54, 55
patriarchy, 100, 139, 143, 144, 145
pelicans, 50
Penguins and Golden Calves, 39, 52,
   55, 56q, 65q, 72, 73q, 101q,
   160q
People Across the Lake, 66-67
People of the Wind, 139
pets, 89, 90, 99
Porter, Calvin L., 43q
Portugal, 33
power, 19, 68-69, 74, 98, 115, 122
prayer, 42, 63, 131, 152-53, 154,
   160
   See also "Jesus Prayer"; L'Engle,
     devotional live of; Lord's
     Prayer; listening
prejudice, 34-35, 123, 132-33, 138
princesses, 177
prism, *See* suncatcher
Proginoskes, 76, 82, 84, 124, 157
Psalms, 46, 48, 55, 61, 152

- R -

racism, *See* prejudice

redemption, 48, 49

Reiner, Stella, 132

resurrection, 36, 48-49, 54, 111,
118, 155

Ring of Endless Light, A, 25, 26, 36,
48, 49q, 62-63q, 75q, 78, 79,
83, 84q, 87q, 90, 91q, 92, 96,
97q, 104, 124, 125-26q, 127q,
146, 147q

rituals, 91, 92, 95, 109, 111, 112
See also liturgy

Rock That Is Higher, The, 39, 45q,
52, 53q, 54q, 55q, 66q, 77,
79q, 80, 81q, 88, 89q, 96q,
99, 109q, 111q, 118q, 121q,
130, 131q, 134q, 144q, 145q,
146q, 151q, 157q, 194n8,
194n29

Rodney, Commander, 62, 126,
127

Rodney, Leo, 62, 127

Rowan, Louisa, 101

- S -

sacrament, 96, 97, 110, 111, 112,
116, 117

sacrifice, 48

salvation, *See* redemption

science, 59, 67, 83, 121-22, 140
See also astrophysics

Scripture, *See* Bible

Senex, 124

Severed Wasp, A, 36, 48, 79, 98,
112, 113, 114q, 115, 119,
129, 130q, 133, 141-42q

Shaw, Luci, 17-20, 22, 40, 41, 102,
116

sin, 43, 78, 79, 152, 153

singing, 25, 47, 59, 64, 83, 85, 87,
91, 95, 97, 126, 155, 156

Small Rain, The, 14, 31q, 36, 88,
113

Smith College, 31, 46, 108
See also L'Engle, Madeleine,
education of

Sold into Egypt, 37, 53q, 54q, 66q,
68, 71q, 81q, 82-83q, 84q,
96q, 124q, 126q, 127-28q,
131q, 138q, 145-46q

Somerville, David, 38, 194n24
See also **Colubra, Bishop Nason**

Sporos, 76, 84-85, 124

St. Hilda's and St. Hugh's School,
33, 34, 112

stars, 35, 57-58, 63, 74, 82, 85, 92,
93, 107, 125, 156, 175

star-watching rock, 72, 92

Stone for a Pillow, A, 37, 54q, 55q,
57q, 63, 66q, 68q, 107q,
118q, 120q, 122q, 123q,
131q, 134-35q, 144q, 148q,
156q

story, 18, 19, 25, 42, 45, 49, 51, 54,
58, 110, 157, 159, 193n17
See also biblical stories; L'Engle,
Madeleine, as a storyteller

*Summer of the Great-grandmother,
The*, 34, 35, 76, 92q, 96q,
132q, 155-56q

suncatcher, 17-19, 20, 43-44,
159-60

Swiftly Tilting Planet, A, 35, 40, 141,
148

*Swiftly Tilting Worlds of Madeleine
L'Engle, The*, 40

symbol, 45, 50, 52, 53, 110, 117,
159

- T -

Tallis, Canon Tom, 34, 192n4
technocracy, 126
tessering, 47, 77
theatre, 39, 108, 109
theology, 25, 27, 33, 47, 58, 67, 110
  See also L'Engle, Madeleine,
    theology of
time, See kairos; chronos
time travel, 47, 64, 65, 139
Time Trilogy, The, 35, 124, 148
trinity, 65, 74, 153
Trinity Episcopal Church, 119
Troubling a Star, 39, 122q, 196n9
truth, 14, 18-19, 20, 45, 53-54, 56,
  68, 81, 111, 159, 193n17
Two-Part Invention, 34, 38, 92,
  98q, 119

- U -

Uncle Douglas, See **Austin, Douglas**
Uncle Hal, See **Huxley, Hal**
Undercroft, Bishop Alwood, 114
unicorns, 47, 50
universe, 54, 56, 57-58, 59, 67, 85,
  110, 111, 121, 126, 132, 146,
  151, 158
  See also interconnectedness;
    interdependence
universe-disturber, 20, 68, 134-35,

- V -

Vaughan, Henry, 62
Vigneras, Justin, 129, 130
Vigneras, Katherine Forrester, 36,
  79, 112, 113, 114, 115, 119,
  129-30, 133, 141-42

- W -

Walking on Water, 25q, 41-43q,
  58q, 141q, 152q, 153q, 158q,
  159q
war, 14, 31, 58, 73, 87, 115, 123,
  124, 125, 128-32, 133, 137,
  143, 145, 158
Weather of the Heart, The, 35q,
  76-77q, 78, 154-55q
web sites, 189-90
West, Canon Edward, 34, 46, 92,
  113, 119, 152
  See also **Tallis, Canon Tom**
Whatsit, Mrs, 33, 47
Wheaton College, 26, 27, 35,
  192n3
Wheaton family, 39, 92, 100, 182
  Wheaton, Abby, 127
  Wheaton, Alice, 92, 127
  Wheaton, David, 39, 92, 100,
    127
  Wheaton, Emma, 39, 48, 92,
    127
Which, Mrs, 33, 47
Who Mrs, 33, 47-48
wholeness, 27, 79-80, 81, 82, 85,
  126, 128, 137, 143, 149, 156,
  158
Wiesel, Elie, 78
Wind in the Door, A, 35, 76, 82q,
  84-85q, 124q, 157q
Winter Song, 40
Winter's Love, A, 32
women/female, 14, 53, 57, 73, 108,
  137-49
  See also feminism
Wrinkle in Time, A, 14, 21, 33, 35,
  37, 41, 47q, 48q, 64, 69, 72,
  76, 77, 78, 81q, 89, 90q, 103,
  104, 134, 139, 141, 148

- X -

Xanthakos family, 100, 183
    Xanthakos, Art, 100, 115
    Xanthakos, Camilla Dickinson,
        39, 67, 78-79, 100, 115, 123,
        128-29, 148
    Xanthakos, Mac, 100, 115
    Xanthakos, Olivia, 100, 133,
        148
    Xanthakos, Raffi, 100-101

- Y -

Young Unicorns, The, 34, 98
Yungblut, John R., 157-58q

CAROLE F. CHASE was born in the Panama Canal Zone where she lived until she came to the United States to attend the College of William and Mary. She taught mathematics in New Jersey public schools before enrolling at the Presbyterian School of Christian Education, where she earned a master's degree in Bible in 1964. She spent five years as a campus minister at Mary Washington College. Subsequently, Carole earned her doctorate in Christian ethics from Duke University and was ordained a minister in the Presbyterian Church. She became a faculty member in the Religious Studies Department at Elon College in North Carolina where she currently holds the rank of professor. She is a published poet.

Her interest in Madeleine L'Engle began in 1984. She knows Madeleine personally, has visited in her home, and was responsible for obtaining a grant that brought Madeleine to Elon College for a lecture series in 1989. She has attended conferences and workshops conducted by Madeleine, delivered a series of lectures about her, read her papers that are collected at Wheaton College in Illinois, and teaches a course at Elon College on the religious dimensions of Madeleine L'Engle's writings.

Most recently, Carole edited a book of daily readings for reflection selected from Madeleine L'Engle's writings, which was published by Harper SanFrancisco in 1996 under the title of *Glimpses of Grace*.

Other Innisfree Press Titles

Blackberry Season: A Time to Mourn, A Time To Heal
    Price   0-931055-93-8 $14.95

Braided Streams: Esther and a Woman's Way of Growing
    Bankson   0-931055-05-9 $12.95

The Bridge to Wholenes: A Feminine Alternative to the Hero Myth
    Raffa   0-931055-88-1 $14.95

The Call of the Soul: Six Stages of Spiritual Development
    Bankson   1-880913-34-8 $13.95

Circle of Stones (10th Anniv Ed.): Woman's Journey to Herself
    Duerk   1-880913-36-4 $13.95

Cloudhand, Clenched Fist: Chaos, Crisis, and the Emergence of Community
    Miller   1-880913-19-4 $15.00

Drawing from the Women's Well: Reflections on the Life Passage of Menopause
    Borton   0-931055-87-3 $11.95

Dream Theatres of the Soul: Empowering the Feminine through Jungian Dreamwork
    Raffa   1-880913-10-0 $15.95

Family Puzzles: A Private Life Made Public
    Weltner   1-880913-23-2 $13.95

Finding Stone: A Quiet Parable and Soul-Work Meditation
    Weber   1-880913-20-8 $12.00

God's Forgotten Daughter: What If Jesus Had Been Woman?
    Schneider-Aker 0-931055-92-X $10.95

Guerrillas of Grace: Prayers for the Battle
    Loder   0-931055-04-0 $14.95

I Asked for Intimacy: Stories of Blessings, Betrayals, and Birthings
    Weems   0-931055-80-6 $12.95

I Sit Listening to the Wind (10th Anniv Ed.): Woman's Encounter within Herself
    Duerk   1-880913-37-2 $13.95

It All Begins with Hope: Patients, Caregivers, and the Bereaved Speak Out
    Jevne   0-931055-83-0 $13.95

The Job Hunter's Spiritual Companion
    Carver   1-880913-30-5 $10.95

Just a Sister Away: A Womanist Vision of Women's Relationships in the Bible
    Weems   0-931055-52-0 $12.95

Keeper of the Night: A Portrait of Life in the Shadow of Death
    Modjeska   1-880913-15-1 $14.95

Other Innisfree Press Titles

Nobody Owns Me: A Celibate Woman Discovers Her Sexual Power
        Rothluebber   1-880913-13-5 $12.95

No Time for Nonsense: Getting Well Against the Odds
        Jevne/Levitan   0-931055-63-6 $13.95

One Anothering, Vol I: Biblical Building Blocks for Small Groups
        Meyer   0-931055-73-3 $12.95

One Anothering, Vol II: Building Spiritual Community in Small Groups
        Meyer   1-880913-35-6 $12.95

Out of the Skin Into the Soul: The Art of Aging
        McNamara/Doherty   0-931055-81-4 $14.95

Raising Peaceful Children in a Violent World
        Cecil   1-880913-16-X $16.95

Rattling Those Dry Bones: Women Changing the Church
        Hagen (ed.)   0-931055-99-7 $16.95

Re-Souled: Spiritual Awakening of a Psychiatrist and his Patient in Alcohol Recovery
        Goodson   0-931055-95-4 $13.95

Return to the Sea: Reflections on Anne Morrow Lindbergh's "Gift from the Sea"
        Johnson   1-880913-24-0 $11.95

Sabbath Sense: A Spiritual Antidote for the Overworked
        Schaper   1-880913-25-9 $11.95

Seasons of Friendship: Naomi and Ruth as a Pattern
        Bankson   0-931055-41-5 $12.95

Seven Times the Sun: Guiding Your Child Through the Rhythms of the Day
        Darian   0-931055-96-2 $15.95

Silence: Making the Journey to Inner Quiet
        Taylor   1-880913-21-6 $13.95

Slow Miracles: Urban Women Fighting for Liberation
        Thompson   1-880913-12-7 $11.95

Spiritual Lemons: Biblical Women, Irreverent Laughter, and Righteous Rage
        Brakeman   1-880913-22-4 $12.95

The Star in My Heart: Experiencing Sophia, Inner Wisdom
        Rupp   0-931055-75-X $11.95

Success Redefined: Notes to a Working Woman
        Giovannoni   1-880913-26-7 $10.95

Suncatcher: A Study of Madeleine L'Engle and Her Writing
        Chase   1-880913-31-3 $15.95

Other Innisfree Press Titles

This Is My Body: Creativity, Clay, and Change
        Bankson   0-931055-94-6 $14.95

To Love Delilah: Claiming the Women of the Bible
        Cartledge-Hayes   0-931055-68-7 $10.95

Tracks in the Straw: Tales Spun from the Manger
        Loder   1-880913-29-1 $12.95

The Voice of Hope: Heard Across the Heart of Life
        Jevne   1-880913-09-7 $13.95

A Weaving of Wonder: Fables to Summon Inner Wisdom
        Brown/Rogers   1-880913-14-3 $12.95

Whole Earth Meditation: Ecology for the Spirit
        Sauro   0-931055-89-X $10.95

The Woman Who Found Her Voice: A Tale of Transforming
        O'Halloran/Delattre   1-880913-18-6 $12.95

The Woman Who Lost Her Heart: A Tale of Reawakening
        O'Halloran/Delattre   1-880913-27-5 $12.95

Wrestling the Light: Ache and Awe in the Human-Divine Struggle
        Loder   0-931055-79-2 $14.95

Writing and Being: Taking Back Our Lives through the Power of Language
        Nelson   1-880913-11-9 $14.95

Innisfree
Press, Inc.

*A call to the
deep heart's core*

*For a Complimentary Catalog
or a copy of our Church Resource Suggestions,
call 1-800-367-5872.*